Computerized Cataloguing

Computerized Cataloguing

ERIC J HUNTER MA FLA AMIET

Senior Lecturer
School of Librarianship and Information Studies
Liverpool Polytechnic

CLIVE BINGLEY LONDON

71491

First published 1985
Reprinted 1986

British Library Cataloguing in Publication Data

Hunter, Eric J.
    Computerized cataloguing.
    1. Descriptive cataloguing—Data processing
    I. Title
    025.3'2'02854   Z694

    ISBN 0-85157-377-0

Contents

Acknowledgements

I am grateful to the following institutions, organizations and services for permission to reproduce their material: Bibliotekstjänsts Utlånings-och Mediakontroll System; BLCMP Library Services Ltd; Bradford Libraries; British Library Bibliographic Services Division; Cheshire Libraries; CL Systems Inc; Farestead Associates; Glasgow University Library; Iowa City Library; Lancashire Polytechnic Library; Liverpool Polytechnic Library; OCLC Europe; Polytechnic of North London Library; Sefton Libraries; SWALCAP; UTLAS Inc; University of California Division of Library Automation; University of Ottawa Library; University of Sussex Library.

Among the individuals who generously gave of their time to advise or otherwise assist are the following: Graham Chan (Liverpool Polytechnic Library); David Goodwin (Cheshire Libraries); Frances Hendrix (Lancashire Polytechnic Library); Alan Jeffreys (University of Newcastle Library); Ray Parry (Liverpool Polytechnic Computer Services Department); John Pemberton (University of Buckingham Library); Ben Tucker (Library of Congress); Jean Weihs (Seneca College of Arts and Technology); Bob Young (University of Sussex Library). Many other people, some of whom are connected with services noted in the first paragraph above, helped in a variety of ways and my thanks are also due to them although it is impossible to mention them all by name.

Certain relevant extracts and illustrations from *Cataloguing* (2nd ed. — Bingley, 1983) have been adapted and amended for use in this text. I am grateful to my co-author of that work, K G B Bakewell, for readily agreeing to their use.

It is important to note that reproductions of screen formats (such as those in use at the University of Sussex Library) are not necessarily to scale and screen images may be compressed.

Author's note

This book is intended as an introduction to a complex and constantly evolving subject. Technological advance is extremely rapid; changes in computer application are common and numerous. Inevitably there will be institutions which will consider that their automated systems should have been mentioned; inevitably there will be important computer cataloguing packages which have been excluded; inevitably any work such as this will be dated, in some respects, as soon as it is written. Apologies are offered, in advance, for any omissions or errors but it is hoped that these will not detract from the work's general aim of providing an outline review of the computer and its use in the cataloguing process, and it is stressed that examples cited in the text are intended merely as illustrations of a wide range of activity.

Because textbooks cannot keep pace with progress, it is essential to read professional journals. A select list of some of the periodicals referred to while this work was being prepared is given below. Those titles marked with an asterisk were particularly useful.

BLAISE newsletter
  Aimed at the operational user of the British Library BLAISE system. Monthly or bi-monthly.
British Library Bibliographic Services Division newsletter
  Four issues a year.
Cataloging and classification quarterly
  Haworth Press.
Cataloging service bulletin
  Issued by the Library of Congress Processing Department. Irregular.
Catalogue & index
  The periodical of the Library Association Cataloguing and Indexing Group. Quarterly.
Database : the magazine of database reference and review
  Online Inc. Four issues per year.
IMP newsletter
  Created by the IFLA International MARC Programme *et al.* as a means of communication for those interested in the development of MARC (especially UNIMARC). Irregular.

The indexer

The journal of the Society of Indexers and of the affiliated American, Australian and Canadian Societies. Twice a year.

Information retrieval and library automation

Newsletter giving details of new techniques, new equipment, new software, events, meetings, etc. Lomond Publications (US). Monthly.

Information technology and libraries*

The official publication of the Library and Information Technology Association, a division of the American Library Association. Quarterly. Formerly *Journal of library automation.*

International cataloguing

The bulletin of the IFLA International Office for UBC (Universal Bibliographic Control). Quarterly.

Library high-tec

A current guide to available and forthcoming technologies applicable to library and information centres. Pierian Press (US). Quarterly.

Library micromation news

News and views for micro users in libraries. IT Centre, Polytechnic of Central London. Quarterly.

Library resources and technical services*

The publication of the Resources and Technical Services Division of the American Librarian Association. Quarterly.

Microcomputers for information management

An international journal for library and information services. Ablex (US). Quarterly.

Online review

The international journal of online information systems. Learned Information (US). Six issues per year.

Program*

Includes news and information of computers in libraries. Aslib (UK). Quarterly.

Technical services quarterly

New trends in computers, automation, and advanced technologies in the operation of libraries and information centres. Haworth Press (US).

VINE*

Provides up-to-date news of work being done in the automation of housekeeping processes. Information

Officer for Library Automation (based at the Polytechnic of Central London from 1 June 1984). Four issues a year.

The above list is restricted to publications specific to cataloguing and/or automation but it should be noted that other more general periodicals relating to librarianship (eg *Australian library journal, Canadian library journal, Library Association record, Library journal, Library of Congress information bulletin*, etc) often contain news and information which is of relevance, as do specialized journals such as *Audiovisual librarian, Electronic library, Information age, Journal of documentation, Videodisc and optical disc* (formerly *Videodisc/videotex*) and the numerous computer magazines which now proliferate.

Additional important sources of up-to-date information are research reports such as those sponsored, in the US, by the Council on Library Resources and undertaken, in the UK, by the Centre for Catalogue Research or by individuals financed by the British Library Research and Development Department.

It should be noted that this text does not set out to cover the general principles and practices of cataloguing and indexing. This is done quite adequately in a number of other works. A few more recent examples are:

Booth, Pat F
   Information filing and finding / Pat F Booth and M L South. – ELM Publications, 1982.
Foskett, A C
   The subject approach to information / A C Foskett. – 4th ed. – Bingley, 1982.
Foster, Donald L
   Managing the catalog department / Donald L Foster. – 2nd ed. – Scarecrow Press, 1982.
Hunter, Eric J
   Cataloguing / Eric J Hunter and K G B Bakewell. – 2nd rev. and expanded ed. – Bingley, 1983.
Wynar, Bohdan S
   Introduction to cataloguing and classification / Bohdan S Wynar, with the assistance of Arlene Taylor Dowell and Jeanne Osborn. – 6th ed. – Libraries Unlimited, 1980.

Glossary

In this glossary are defined selected terms which are also explained in the text and some other terms which are not referred to in the text but for which the computer user may at some time require an explanation. The glossary is not intended to be exhaustive.

Access point: a term under which an item is likely to be sought in a catalogue or bibliography.

Access time: the time taken by a computer to obtain information from its backing store.

Acoustic coupler: means of connecting a computer or terminal to the telephone system without an electrical connection. The handset fits into two rubber cups on the coupler. *See also* Modem.

Address: a means of locating data (qv) in a store (qv) — analogous to the unique address of a house within a town.

Algorithm: an ordered set of well-defined rules for solving a problem within a finite number of steps.

Array: a set of values or variables that collectively are referred to by a single name. Individual members of the set are identified by a SUBSCRIPT. For example. AUTHOR$(5), in BASIC (qv), identifies the fifth entry in the array or list AUTHOR$.

ASCII: American Standard Code for Information Interchange, a common method of ranking characters in a numeric order of value.

Assembler: colloquial term for assembly language which lies between the low-level machine code (qv) and high-level languages (*see* Programming languages). Assembler is a mnemonic code using symbols which the processor can quickly convert to machine code.

Authority file: a file which indicates the accepted form of an access point (qv).

Automatic data processing (ADP): the manipulation of data by a computer.

Back-up: a spare copy of computer programs or data.

Backing store: the immediate access store (qv) is limited in capacity and, in smaller computers, it may need to be cleared before a new set of instructions is entered. A backing or secondary store, which will provide additional storage on magnetic tapes, discs, etc, is therefore required.

Bar-code label: data encoded on a label as a series of thick and thin lines. When a light sensitive 'pen' is passed over the label the pattern of lines is detected electrically.

BASIC: Beginner's All-purpose Symbolic Instruction Code. The great attraction of BASIC as a programming language (qv) is that it is easily learned. It is the resident language in many of the small personal computers which are now on the market.

Batch processing: jobs held back until there are sufficient to process in a group or batch. *See also* Offline.

Baud: a measurement of the speed at which data can be transmitted by a terminal (qv). Slow terminals operate at speeds up to 300 baud, faster terminals at 1,200 baud or even more. A baud can be roughly equated to one bit per second which means that 300 baud is approximately 30 characters per second.

Binary system: a numbering system with a base of two which when written appear as a series of 0's and 1's. The computer can only 'recognize' two states 'on' or 'off', ie a 'pulse' or 'no pulse', a 'hole' or 'no hole'. The binary system therefore forms the basis of computer operation.

A **binary digit** is one of the characters from the set 0 and 1. A binary digit is also known as a **bit**.

Binary coded decimals eliminate the necessity to convert from decimal to pure binary. Each decimal digit is treated separately. For example, the number 215 would be represented by:

    0 0 1 0 / 0 0 0 1 / 0 1 0 1

Bit: a binary digit. *See under* Binary system.

Boolean logic: in information retrieval, the use of the Boolean operators AND, OR or NOT to combine search terms in order to produce a more precise statement of the search requirement.

Boot: to start up a computer system.

Bubble memory: a recent development where each individual memory element is a magnetic 'bubble' formed on a thin slice of a magnetic crystal by an applied magnetic field. Bubble memories are intended as cheap, bulk stores.

Bug: an error in a program or an equipment malfunction.

Bus: the set of signal wires or printed circuit board tracks through which a computer communicates with its own internal components or with external equipment.

Byte: the number of bits (usually eight) needed to store a single character. The capacity of the immediate access store associated with a microcomputer will normally be presented in terms of bytes. For example, a 48K store consists of approximately 48,000 × 8 bits or 48,000 bytes and thus it will hold 48,000 characters. *See also* Word.

Card reader: a machine which can interpret the information on a punched card (qv) and input it to the computer.

Central processing unit (CPU): the heart of the computer — that part which contains the electronic circuits of the arithmetic and control units.

Character: a single symbol that the computer can 'recognize' such as a letter (A–Z), number (0–9), punctuation mark, etc. A 'space' is also a character to the computer.

CIM (Computer Input Microform): a method of interpreting information in microform and inputting it to the computer. Uses optical characters (qv).

Chip: *see under* Computer.

CIP: Cataloguing In Publication. The provision of cataloguing information within a published document. CIP data may also appear in machine-readable form to give early warning of the document's publication, eg in an online database.

COBOL: Common Business Oriented Language. A useful programming language (qv) for library applications.

COM (Computer Output Microform): machine readable output from a computer is automatically converted into microform (microfilm or microfiche). This has distinct advantages over conventional printed output from the points of view of cost and bulk.

Compiler: a program for converting a high-level language such as BASIC or COBOL (qv) into a machine format which the computer can understand. *See also* Programming language.

Computer: a machine (today the term 'computer' usually refers to an electronic machine) which will carry out complex calculations or 'clerical' operations at fantastic speeds.

A **basic computer** comprises an arithmetic unit (to perform the calculations), a store or memory (to contain instructions and data) and a control unit (to coordinate operations and carry out the instructions contained in a program). *See also* Central processing unit.

Peripherals include input and output devices and, as the immediate access store has a limited capacity, backing or secondary storage on magnetic tape or disc, etc.

A **'mainframe'** computer is a large computer which is required to run a number of different processing tasks at the same time.

'Mini-computers' are more compact, lower priced computers, which nevertheless still offer a high degree of versatility.

The development of the **'micro-computer'**, built around the **silicon chip** (an electronic circuit comprising many separate inter-connected components manufactured as a single integrated unit) has revolutionized the computer industry.

When a basic computer (see above) is integrated on one silicon chip, it is known as a **'microprocessor'** – the functional equivalent of a central processing unit (CPU) in the traditional large computer. The microprocessor is used with other (often integrated) components to form a micro-computer.

Irrespective of size, a computer configuration must comprise a central processing unit, a storage unit and input/output units. The differences between micros, minis and mainframes are mainly concerned with internal complexity, relative speed, the amount of data that can be transmitted in a given time, and hence cost.

Configuration: a general term used to refer to the physical components of a computer system.

Connect time: the amount of time that elapses whilst a user is connected online (qv) to a computer system.

Control number: a unique number used to identify an item, eg the ISBN (qv), or an LC (Library of Congress) or BNB (British National Bibliography) number.

Core store: *see under* Magnetic storage. Also used generally to refer to the immediate access store (qv) but, strictly, this is only correct when the immediate access store *is* a core store. This would not be so, for example, in a micro-computer.

CPS: characters per second. A measurement of the speed at which information is displayed on a screen or printed by a printer.

CPU: *see* Central processing unit.

CPU time: the time taken by the computer to process a set of instructions. This will be considerably less than the actual connect time (qv).

CRT: cathode ray tube. A CRT terminal is American terminology for a visual display unit (qv).

Current awareness: a search for the latest material on a particular subject. *See also* SDI.

Cursor: a spot of light or other symbol, eg a question mark, on the screen of a visual display unit that indicates where the next character to be displayed will appear.

Daisywheel: *see under* Printer.

Data: the information to be processed by the computer.

Database: a collection of records (qv) is referred to as a file (qv) and a database consists of one or more files.

Debug: the location and removal of errors from a program. *See also* Bug.

Dedicated line: a telephone line which is reserved for the connection of a terminal directly to a computer.

Default: a predetermined value or option automatically assumed by the machine when none has been supplied by the operator.

Diagnostic: printout from the computer for checking.

Direct access: relates to the way in which a read/write head can go straight to the location of data (as on magnetic disc). Also referred to as random access. Compare with 'serial' access (as on magnetic tapes) when all of the tape preceding a particular item must be run through before the item is reached.

Disc (disk): *see under* Magnetic storage.

Diskette: sometimes used to refer to the smaller 5¼ in or 8 in diameter floppy disc.

Display: visible representation of data as on a visual display unit (qv).

Distributed catalogue: a system in which the catalogue is made available at numerous remote locations, thus placing the data nearer to the user. The online (qv) catalogue offers the most potential in this area, with access being possible even from the comfort of one's own home.

Dot matrix: *see under* Printer.

Down: a computer is said to be 'down' when it ceases to function for some reason.

Download: to capture data online from a remote host computer and transfer it to the store of an in-house stand-alone system, eg a microcomputer, for processing. This can save connect and telecommunication costs. The reverse is to **upload.**

Drum: *see under* Magnetic storage.

Duplex: a term used in relation to the transmission and display of characters at a terminal (qv). With 'half duplex' each character is displayed at the terminal as it is transmitted. With 'full duplex' each character is transmitted to the computer and then echoed back to the terminal for display.

EMMA: Extra-MARC MAterial. Records created by outside agencies, ie other than the British Library or the Library of Congress, when no record is present in the MARC (qv) databases.

Fibre optics: an enormously fast and highly reliable form of telecommunication transmission line in which a light wave is sent along a thin strand of glass. It is claimed (British Telecom) that the whole of the *Encyclopaedia Britannica* could be transmitted in half a second.

Field: a sub-division of a record (qv) for a particular type of information, for example the 'author' field or the 'title' field within a catalogue record. The number of characters in a field can be variable or fixed. A 'fixed' field is a field of specified length, ie limited to a certain number of characters. A 'variable' length field may contain a varying number of characters; its beginning and end must be indicated by specified tags.

File: a collection of related and usually similarly constructed records (qv) treated as a unit, eg the catalogue of a library.

Fixed field: *see under* Field.

Floppy disc: a circular piece of thin, flexible, coated plastic with a magnetic recording surface. Common sizes are

5¼ in and 8 in diameter. The disc is placed in a disc drive when required for use. *See also* Hard disc and Magnetic storage.

Flow chart: a diagrammatic representation of a flow of operations. Below is shown a very simple example of a flowchart for the input of a series of document titles. Input can continue until the rogue string 'ZZZ' is entered. The number of titles are counted as they are input, the total being equal to C:

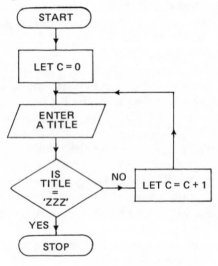

The flowchart symbols used in the above diagram are:

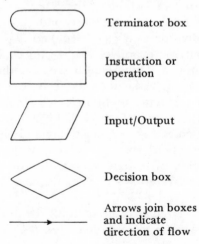

Terminator box

Instruction or operation

Input/Output

Decision box

Arrows join boxes and indicate direction of flow

There are a number of other standard symbols which are used to represent the sequence of operations and the flow of data for programming and systems flowcharts. Where programming is concerned, however, some languages now use structure diagrams in preference to flowcharts. *See also* Structured programming.

Format: the arrangement or presentation of data in a machine-readable record.

Hard copy: eye-readable output on paper, card, etc.

Hard disc: a rigid disc fixed permanently into a disc drive. An efficient method of storing large amounts of programs and data, which is faster, more reliable and much more capacious than the floppy disc (qv). *See also* Magnetic storage and Winchester disc.

Hardware: the physical components of a computer system.

Hexadecimal: a numbering system to base sixteen that uses the numbers 0—9 and letters A—F. The use of a hexadecimal keyboard facilitates the entry of instructions in machine code. For example, the machine code binary instruction 0001 1001 could be entered as 1 9.

High-level language: *see under* Programming language.

Hit: the finding of a record which matches a search request.

Host: a main computer, being accessed via terminals (qv) and/or mini/microcomputers.

Housekeeping: looking after a particular system.

Immediate access store: the central store or memory of a computer. *See also* Backing store; Computer; Core store; Magnetic storage.

Input: the data to be read into a computer system *or* the process of reading the data into the system.

Intelligent terminal: a terminal equipped with an immediate access store and a CPU (qv) so that it is capable of processing data independently to a limited extent.

Interactive: a mode of online (qv) interaction between the user and a computer system.

Interface: the connection between two systems or two parts of the same system.

IPSS: International Packet Switching Service. A telecommunications network using packet switching (qv) available between the US, UK and other countries.

ISBN: International Standard Book Number. A unique number allocated to each book published so that computerization in the book trade is facilitated.

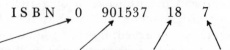

ISBN   0   901537   18   7

Group identifier	Publisher identifier	Title identifier	Check digit
'0' = English speaking countries (UK, USA, Canada, Eire, Australia, South Africa)	'901537' = School of Librarianship and Information Studies, Liverpool Polytechnic	'18' = the nine-teenth item (with an ISBN) published by the School	A device that guards against the computer accepting a 'wrong number'

K: 1,000, an abbreviation for Kilo (more specifically 2^{10} = 1024).

Line printer: *see under* Printer.

Logical operators: *see under* Boolean logic.

Login: procedure for gaining access to a **time sharing** (qv) system.

Logoff: procedure for leaving a computer system.

Loop: a sequence of instructions in a program which is designed to be repeated as many times as is required.

Machine code: the most fundamental programming language (qv). Instructions are written in binary coding, ie as an organized sequence of '0's and '1's.

Machine readable: a record capable of being read by a machine, eg a computer.

Magnetic characters: characters printed with an ink contain-ing magnetic material. A 'font' has to be devised so that each character gives a different signal when passed under a reading head.

Magnetic characters

Magnetic storage: any machine-readable form of storage which utilizes the properties of magnetism. 'Core' stores were common at one time. These consisted of rings or cores and every ring was capable of being magnetized in one of two states to represent either a binary 1 or 0. The immediate access store of most computer systems today is more likely to be electronic and consist of silicon chips. Secondary magnetic stores such as cards, discs, drums or tapes are coated with a material which can be magnetized. Data are recorded by the presence or absence of a magnetic spot.

Magnetic cards: a similar shape but somewhat bigger than punched cards. They usually present a solid black surface and cannot be 'read' visually.

Magnetic discs: discs up to three feet in diameter which rotate at very high speeds. The flat surface of each disc is covered with closely packed tracks of magnetic spots. These spots can be produced or interpreted by read/write heads which can select any required track with an access time of a fraction of a second.

Magnetic drums offer similar facilities to the disc but each drum consists of a cylinder with parallel tracks of magnetic spots around its circumference.

Magnetic tape: a long strip of coated plastic material usually containing seven or nine tracks or channels. Magnetic tapes are a very successful storage device, offering high speeds, compactness, low cost and an ability to re-use, but they have one big disadvantage in that all of the tape preceding a required item must be run before the item is reached. Access time can, therefore, be quite long. Discs and drums, on the other hand, provide the facility of direct access (qv) where the time needed to access an item is independent of the location of the item in the store.

Mainframe: *see under* Computer.

MARC: MAchine Readable Cataloguing.

Memory: *see* Store.

Menu: a list of options shown on a vdu screen.

Micro-computer and Mini-computer: *see under* Computer.

Microprocessor: a component in a micro-computer. *See under* Computer.

Modem: the linking device between a terminal and a telephone line; the signal transmitted over the line is converted into a form suitable for the terminal and vice versa. 'Modem' is a contraction of 'modulator-demodulator'. *See also* Acoustic coupler.

Monitor: *see under* Visual display unit.

Node: a point of access to a telecommunications network.

Offline: relates to 'batch mode', operating without direct and continuous communication with the main computer system. *See also* Online.

Online: a system in which there is direct communication with the central processing unit of a computer, allowing an operator to 'converse' directly with the computer and receive an almost immediate response to a message or instruction. Online is to offline as the telephone is to the postal service. *See also* Offline.

Operating system: the set of internal programs which make up the control system of the computer itself.

Optical character recognition: a method by which printed characters can be 'read' by a computer; a light-sensitive machine converts the print into electrical impulses which can be stored in machine readable form.

Optical disc: *see under* Videodisc.

Packet switching: the transmission of messages through a communication network.

Paper tape: *see* Punched tape.

PASCAL: a high-level programming language (qv) which is very flexible and which can be implemented on some microcomputers.

Peripherals: input and output devices, backing store, etc of a computer system.

PL1: a high-level programming language (qv) which is useful for library applications.

Print-out: the output of a printer on a paper roll or continuous stationery.

Printer: prints output from the computer usually onto paper. A 'line printer' prints one line at a time at very high speed, eg 1,500 lines per minute, and uses 'continuous' stationery. Smaller printers may be of different types. A daisywheel printer has a wheel to do the actual printing which looks like a daisy and which has a character at the end of each 'petal'. A matrix printer forms characters as required by means of dots, ie dot matrix. The impact dot matrix uses a print head of needles which are independently controlled to strike a ribbon onto paper. This is the most common type of microcomputer printer. Non-impact printers include the thermal matrix printer which uses miniature heat elements to form the dots and the expensive (£9,000–£30,000) but very fast and superior laser printer, which works in a somewhat similar way to an electrostatic photocopier.

Procedure: an instructional part of a written program, a sub-program, *or* any course of action taken for the solution of a problem.

Procedure acceptance: *see under* Systems analysis.

Program: a sequence of instructions to enable the computer to carry out a particular task.

Programming language: the language in which a program is written.

Programming in a machine-code is time-consuming, laborious and requires a highly trained person. However, intermediate 'high-level' languages have been devised to facilitate the process. Examples are BASIC (qv); COBOL (qv); PL1 (Programming Language 1) (qv); FORTRAN (FORmula TRANslation; and PASCAL (qv);

The program written in a high-level langauge is translated, within the machine, by a master program (the compiler) into machine code.

PSS: Packet Switching Service. A packet switching (qv) network operated in the UK by British Telecom. *See also* IPSS.

Punched cards: pieces of card of specified size in which holes are punched in columns according to a code in order to represent data. A standard card has 80 columns and will therefore hold up to 80 characters. Cards can be 'read' into a computer at speeds of up to 1,500 cards per minute. *See also* Punched tape.

Punched tape: a long strip of paper upon which holes are punched. Each row of holes across the tape represents a character in accordance with a specified code. There may be 5, 6, 7 or 8 tracks or channels. Paper tape can be input at speeds of up to 1,000 characters per second. Punched tape character sets can include upper and lower case letters, unlike punched cards which are limited to capitals. Punched tape is inexpensive and it is impossible to get data out of order. It is, however, less flexible than cards; it cannot be read visually and is difficult to amend. *See also* Punched cards.

RAM: Random-Access Memory.

Random access: *see* Direct access.

Real time: computer operations keeping pace with the process. For example, in the process of landing an aircraft 'blind', conditions constantly change and it must be possible for the necessary changes in the aircraft controls to be computed and a correction applied in time for this to be of value.

Record: the complete set of information relating to a particular item in a file. Each record consists of one or more fields.

Relational database: a more recent type of database in which data manipulation commands relate records in different files on the basis of data values rather than by explicit pointers.

Relational operator: a symbol representing 'greater than', 'less than', or 'equal to', ie >, <, or =.

Remote access: access to a computer by means of a terminal which may be located some distance away.

ROM: Read-Only Memory.

Screen format: the layout of the information displayed on the screen of a vdu (qv).

SDI: Selective Dissemination of Information. A regular updating service which alerts clients in relation to recent information on specific subjects. *See also* Current awareness.

Secondary store: *see* Backing store.

Serial access: the opposite of direct access (qv).

Silicon chip: *see under* Computer.

Software: all of the programs used to instruct the computer and the associated documentation.

Sort: to arrange data in ascending or descending order, either numerically or alphabetically.

Store: a device for holding programs or data which allows them to be used and retrieved as required. *See also* Backing store; Core store; Magnetic storage.

String: a sequence of characters (qv).

Structured programming: the breaking down of complex problems into more conceptually manageable sub-problems, which may, in turn, be broken down into sub-sub-problems and so on. This process of structuring terminates when a set of constituent sub-problems has been derived for which methods of solution can be formulated.

Subroutine: a section of a program (qv) which may be needed more than once. By placing it in a subroutine, it can be called up as required. *See also* Procedure.

Subscript: *see under* Array.

Systems analysis: commonly used to cover all aspects involved

in ensuring that a computerized system works effectively
and with maximum possible efficiency. Systems analysis
is not solely concerned with computers but is associated
more with those situations likely to require a computer
than with any others.

It includes the following stages:

1 System analysis
   (The more specific meaning of the term)
   The examination of an existing method of controlling an activity in order to ascertain whether computerization might lead to an improvement.

2 System design
   The planning of a new way of doing a job or of improving an existing system.

3 System implementation
   The installation and testing of a new system to ensure
   that it does what is required.
   Procedure acceptance is that stage in system implementation when the proposed computer operation has been
   proved successful in a test run.

4 System maintenance
   Striving to maintain and improve a system so that it
   always achieves maximum efficiency for minimum
   expenditure.

Systems definition: The formal specification of the principles
and detailed procedures of the final working system of a
computer operation.

Tag: a symbol used to identify a particular field or element
in a record.

Terminal: a device used to communicate with a computer
system. An 'intelligent' terminal (qv) is a terminal which
can be programmed or instructed to automatically carry
out certain operations.

Time sharing: servicing of a number of terminals by one
computer almost simultaneously.

Trapping store: a device used to indicate availability of an
item in demand.

Truncation: the shortening of a search term so that it will
match any term starting (front truncation) or finishing
(back truncation) with the same stem, eg: COMPUT. . will
match COMPUTER, COMPUTING, etc; . . LIOTT will
match ELIOTT or ELLIOTT.

Turnkey package: a complete computer system comprising hardware and software (qv) together with service and support.

Upload: *see under* Download.

User-friendliness: the ability of an automated system to allow interaction with a user without difficulty.

Validation: a means of ensuring that the data input is correct.

Variable length field: *see under* Field.

Videodisc: the generic term encompasses both the 'entertainment' type videodisc and the information oriented optical disc. Both can provide high capacity secondary storage and it is possible for the personal computer enthusiast to make use of a home video recorder in this way. The optical disc, however, which is created by a laser beam burning small holes in a reflective surface, is of much greater significance as a storage medium offering ten to one hundred times the digital capacity of a magnetic disc of similar size and enabling whole collections of complete documents to be stored and speedily retrieved.

Virtual storage: a method of memory management that allows a computer's operating system to act as if there is more internal storage capacity than there actually is. Only small sections of a program or data file may be needed in this store at any one time, the remainder may be kept in an adjacent extremely fast direct access storage device and fed in or out portion by portion by the operating system as required. Execution will take place as if all of the program or data were continually held in the internal store.

Visual display unit (vdu): a unit used to display data from a computer onto a screen. It may have a keyboard attached so that data may be input, output or edited. Without the keyboard the vdu is often referred to as a monitor.

Winchester disc: a common type of sealed hard disc (qv) unit for use with a microcomputer. *See also* Magnetic storage.

Word: a group of bits (qv) treated as a unit which normally holds one item of data or one instruction. Very similar to byte (qv) but usually longer, eg 24 bits, and used more with mini or mainframe computers.

Word processor: a device for manipulating and repositioning textual matter automatically. It is intended to improve productivity by avoiding the need to 're-type' material which has already been set-up correctly.

Chapter One

Why use a computer?

Definition of cataloguing

A *catalogue* is a list of, and index to, a collection of materials. It enables the user to discover:

 a What material is present in the collection
 b Where this material may be located.

The 'collection' may relate to one or a number of library or information service points. In the latter case, the catalogue is termed a *union catalogue*.

The catalogue has much in common with the *bibliography*, which is also a list of books and/or other material. The same principles are applied to their compilation and they are used interchangeably. For example, the British Museum *General catalogue of printed books* or the various Library of Congress catalogues also act as important bibliographies. The latter represent the most comprehensive current bibliographic service in the world to English speaking countries but they are still the catalogues of a specific collection. The pure bibliography is not an index to a specific collection but rather a list of material within a restricted field, perhaps relating to a specific subject, or published in a particular country or a particular language.

The art (or perhaps it should be the science) of *cataloguing* therefore relates to both catalogues *and* bibliographies. It is the art of describing and listing material in such a way as to make it as easy as possible to discover the nature and extent of what is available and, if appropriate, where this material may be located or obtained.

Why use a computer?

Contemporary society has experienced an extraordinary explosion in knowledge which has resulted in a corresponding increase in the publication of books and other materials which act as information carriers. In general terms, it is now impractical, if not impossible, to ascertain what material and information exists, and where it may be obtained, without the aid of technology. Production of the *British national bibliography*, for instance, has been computerized for many years. More specifically, in the case of a particular library or information service, technology can be of considerable help in aiding and improving cataloguing techniques.

Computers can process vast amounts of information or data, at great speed and it is these two factors, capacity and speed, which constitute the major reason for computer use:

Capacity Computers can process much more information than would be possible manually, or, put another way, process the same amount of information more cheaply.

Speed Computers can perform clerical operations much faster and more accurately than can a person. Operations that could take many man/hours can be done by the machine in minutes. Information can also be extracted, or accessed, much more quickly and efficiently.

The cataloguing process basically consists of two operations, firstly the creation of the appropriate record relating to an individual item and, secondly, the subsequent manipulation of this and other records to form the actual catalogue:

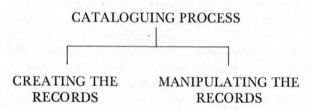

CATALOGUING PROCESS

CREATING THE   MANIPULATING THE
RECORDS   RECORDS

The computer cannot replace the first of these, that intellectual element which only a human being can, at present, supply. A question such as: 'Who is the person responsible for this item?' cannot be answered by a machine, nor can a machine distinguish, for instance, between an author, eg Charles Dickens, and a title, eg David Copperfield.

However, the computer is capable of performing the various

clerical functions involved in the manipulation of records. For example, the computer can quickly *sort* catalogue entries into any desired order, or *search* for records which conform to a particular search profile. And the search facility that can be provided is a much more flexible one than would be possible in a manual index.

Because the computer offers such capabilities as indicated, namely capacity, speed, accuracy and flexibility, it is reasonable to conclude that automation of the cataloguing process could save time, save staff, and hence save money. In theory, this is true and these are obviously major reasons for computerization but, in practice, staff may merely be redeployed. It would be difficult, for instance, to save staff in a 'one-person' library, although staff *time* might be saved. Saving money may also be problematic, especially with the high initial cost of computer equipment. The computer can, however, help to reduce the *rate of increase* in costs.

Fortunately, the computer offers numerous other advantages. It will facilitate extended and higher standards of service, with better control, improved efficiency and higher productivity. In addition, it permits fuller and wider co-operation between libraries and information services.

The objectives of computerized cataloguing may therefore be summarized as follows:[1]

1 To save money, or at least to reduce the rate of increase in costs.
2 To provide better control and improve efficiency.
3 To achieve higher productivity.
4 To extend the service offered.
5 To permit increased co-operation with other libraries or information services.

And all of these objectives are possible because of the computer's appetite for work and the rapidity with which it completes any task that it is given.

Leaving aside objective no 1 for the moment, let us examine some examples of how the above aims have actually been achieved in practice:

1 Adapted from the reasons for automation cited in: Computer-based housekeeping systems / J. Eyre *In Handbook of special librarianship and information work* / editor L.J. Anthony. — 5th ed. — Aslib, 1982 182-203

2 Computerization has enabled many libraries to integrate various activities such as book-ordering, cataloguing and circulation. This has certainly resulted in better control and improved efficiency.

3 Computerized catalogues are usually much more up to date than the manual catalogues that they have replaced; higher productivity has therefore been achieved.

4 Many computerized catalogues offer facilities which were not present previously. A common, if surprising, example is a subject approach, a very necessary extension of the service offered.

5 A standardized format for machine-readable data has provided an unprecedented opportunity for the sharing of the cataloguing activity, for the exchange of bibliographic records, and for vastly increased co-operation possibilities.

To return to objective no 1, it is clear that examples such as that cited in 5 above, namely the sharing of the work involved in cataloguing, might be of considerable economic benefit to the participants.

The computer is a servant not the master but it is a tremendously powerful and willing servant. With its aid the catalogue can also become a very powerful facility. The computer cannot and should not be ignored by any progressive cataloguer. Those librarians who maintain that their manual catalogues and indexes could not be improved by computerization are living in the past.

The efficient and effective use of new technology can, in addition, help to improve the librarian's image and this can only be good for the profession.

Remember too that the computer encourages the creative and innovative urge. In order to make full use of it, one must look beyond the restrictions of traditional cataloguing theory. Start afresh, think anew; the frontiers are boundless.

Chapter Two

What is a computer?

Definition

The word computer derives from the Latin 'computare,' meaning to reckon or compute. Computers were, in fact, originally developed for performing numerical calculations and they are still used for this purpose today. However, computing is no longer confined to numbers. *Any information which can be encoded numerically is potentially open to computer techniques.*

The librarian is concerned primarily with textual information, which is made up of individual characters, ie letters, spaces, punctuation marks, digits and other symbols. It is quite easy to encode such information numerically. For example, A could be represented by 1, B by 2, C by 3, etc, so that Z would be represented by 26. A space could be represented by 27, a full stop by 28, a comma by 29 and so on. In this way any character could be referred to by a number. The computer actually works in this manner, although the example given above is not a realistic one.

It is also possible to encode visual information numerically by dividing the 'picture' into tiny pieces and using a grid, ie a system of numbered squares, as a reference. Here is such a grid; shown after an instruction has been received to fill in squares 0–3, 0–4, 1–2, 1–3, 1–4, 1–5, 2–1, 2–2, etc.

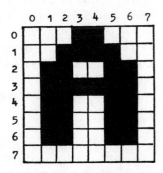

This illustrates how a 'picture' of the letter A can be produced. Thus letters can be 'printed' on the screen of a computer's display unit. Anything 'visual,' for example the space ships, missiles and other ingredients of computer games are 'drawn' in this way. If colour is required, this can also be encoded.

The computer might therefore be defined as: 'a machine capable of receiving, storing, manipulating and outputting information'; with the term *information* encompassing anything which can be encoded numerically.

One word must be added before the above definition is acceptable, viz 'electronic'; the computer of today is an *electronic* machine.

Evolution

The evolution of computer theory can be traced back to the beginning of recorded history and basic concepts were established before the requisite technology became available. However, the real practical breakthrough came following the Second World War when machines were developed using the then new technology of electronics. The first generation of electronic computers used 'glass bottle' type valves. 'Valves,' because, as the name suggests, they either permitted the flow of an electron current or prevented it. Thus the valve acted as a switch but an *electronic* switch which was much faster and more efficient than its mechanical or electro-mechanical equivalent. We shall see why this is important in a moment. Such valves required a great deal of power, generated an excessive amount of heat (each valve having a hot filament) and occupied an enormous amount of space. An early Ferranti computer (1950) contained 4,000 valves, had six miles of wiring, 100,000 soldered joints, and needed 27 Kilowatts of power before it could function. A computer of this era could fill a room. This Ferranti machine filled two bays each 16 feet long by 4 feet deep by 8 feet high.[1]

Then came the transistor and the second generation of computers. The transistor functioned in the same way as the 'glass bottle' valve but it used much less power, generated much less heat and was much smaller. It was also 'solid state' and therefore less fragile, not to mention cheaper.

1 *Information technology revolution* / Robert Irvine Smith, Bob Campbell. — Longman. 1981 15

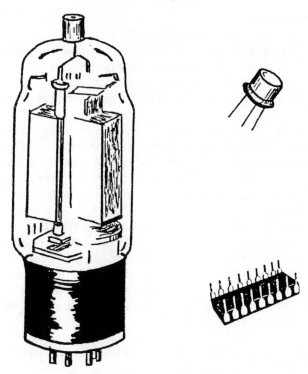

Sketch illustrating appearance and approximate relative size of valve, transistor and microchip

About 1960, the technology was developed for forming the transistors, other components, and their connecting wires into an 'integrated' circuit placed on one small, flat piece of silicon. The pieces, or 'slices' of silicon, with their integrated circuits, became more and more compact and more and more complex. The progress that was made can be measured by the fact that in 1963 it was possible to fit only eight transistors on a slice or 'chip' and yet by 1980 many thousands could be accommodated. By this time, for instance, Ferranti had developed a microprocessor (Europe's first) which was only ¼ inch square but one hundred times more powerful and much more reliable than their first computer mentioned earlier.[1] The third generation of computers had arrived; the 'microchip' revolution had begun.

1 *Information technology revolution* / Robert Irvine Smith, Bob Campbell *op. cit.* 15

Binary system

So far we have learned two basic facts:

    1 Any information which can be encoded numerically is suitable for processing by computer.

    2 The computer is an electronic machine.

How are these facts inter-related and what is their importance?

Being an *electronic* machine, the computer, in essence, can do one thing and one thing only; it can recognize the difference between the two states 'on' and 'off', a current which is flowing or which is not, a switch which is closed or which is open, rather like a person being able to tell whether a light is on or off.

It cannot therefore 'read' numbers such as 1, 2, 5 or 27, ie decimal numbers. If, however, numbers could be presented to the computer in terms of *two* digits only, a '0' for 'off' and a '1' for 'on', then it would be capable of understanding them. Such a numeric system does exist, the 'binary' system, which works to the base two and which, when written, appears as a series of 0s and 1s.

BINARY	SWITCH	PULSE	HOLE
0			
1			●

In the decimal system, which works to the base ten, there must be a total of ten in a column before 1 is carried across. In binary, every time there is a total of *two* in a column, 1 is carried across, eg:

BINARY		DECIMAL		BINARY		DECIMAL
1	=	1		... 101	=	5
+ 1				+ 1		
10	=	2		110	=	6
+ 1				+ 1		
11	=	3		111	=	7
+ 1				+ 1		
100	=	4		1000	=	8
+ 1				+ 1		
101	=	5 ...		1001	=	9
				+ 1		
				1010	=	10

This does, of course, mean that binary numbers are much longer than their decimal equivalents, eg:

10000001100100 = 8292

but, although this is awkward for a person, this makes no difference to the machine with its great capacity and tremendous speed. In any case it is possible to use a shorthand form of binary coded decimals, eg:

1000 / 0010 / 1001 / 0010 = 8292

It can be deduced from the above that:

1 INFORMATION must be stored in the computer in binary form.

2 INSTRUCTIONS must be given to the computer in binary form.

Herein lies the link between the electronic machine and the necessity for numerically encoded information.

A typical instruction to a computer might be:

00001000

which could mean 'Subtract 1 from the total.'

If the instruction is input to the computer in a 'near English' form, which is, as we shall see, perfectly possible, eg

SUBTRACT 1 FROM TOTAL

then this *must* be translated into pure binary, within the machine, before the computer can understand it.

Memory (storage)

The storage capacity of a computer is also related to binary. It is measured by the number of off/ons, ie 0 / 1s, that can be accommodated. The digits 0 and 1 are known as *binary digits* or *bits*. Storage is usually referred to in terms of a combination of bits, for example a 'byte' equals eight bits. Each byte will hold one character or one instruction. Storage is normally presented as so many K, where K is roughly 1000 (actually 1024). A 48K microcomputer would therefore have an internal memory of 48,000 bytes (48,000 × 8 bits), or 48,000 characters. This seems vast but it must hold not only data but also instructions and various other elements required by the computer for efficient operation.

To illustrate just how small a 48K memory actually is, let us examine how much storage might be required to hold a library catalogue. The average size of a catalogue record might be 250 characters. If the library has a stock of ten thousand items then the full catalogue would consist of

```
0 0 0 1 1 0 0 0
0 0 1 1 1 1 0 0
0 1 1 0 0 1 1 0
0 1 1 1 1 1 1 0
0 1 1 0 0 1 1 0
0 1 1 0 0 1 1 0        Bit pattern showing how the letter
0 1 1 0 0 1 1 0        A illustrated on page 5 might be
0 0 0 0 0 0 0 0        built up in binary terms
```

$250 \times 10,000 = 2,500,000$, ie 2,500K characters or, in computer terms, bytes. The catalogue is hardly likely to fit into a 48K store!

It follows that it is necessary to have some form of back-up, or secondary, store to supplement the computer's primary, internal memory. Currently this is most likely to be magnetic disk or magnetic tape.

The actual way in which binary digits may be stored within the computer varies. 'Core' stores were common at one time. These consisted of a large number of ferrite rings or cores each about the size of a typewriter '0'. Every ring was capable of being magnetized in one of two states.

The immediate access store of most computer systems today is more likely to be electronic and made up of silicon chips. There are two types of memory chip known as Read Only Memory (ROM) and Random Access Memory (RAM). ROM is so-called because you can 'read' or get things out of it but you cannot 'write' to it or put things in. With RAM you can read from it or write to it. Thus ROM is used for instructions permanently available on the machine, whilst RAM is used to store instructions and data input by the user. RAM usually needs a constant power supply to retain its contents; when the computer is switched off, the instructions and data are lost.

The backing store may simply operate on a 'hole' or 'no hole' principle, as with punched cards or punched tape, or utilize the properties of magnetism. Discs, tapes, etc are coated with a material which can be magnetized. Data is recorded by the presence or absence of a magnetic 'spot'.

The search for further methods of cheap, bulk storage continues. For example, the so-called 'bubble' memory has been developed. Each individual memory element is a magnetic bubble formed on a thin slice of a magnetic crystal by an applied magnetic field.

One form of backing store which will be of immense value to the librarian is the videodisc, particularly the optical disc. Such discs have tremendous capacities and it is possible to store, in digital form, the actual visual content of various materials, eg slides, photographs, etc, and display this content on a screen as required.

Computer configuration
So much for the store of a computer but this is only one component of the full system.

Firstly, there must be some means of inputting information to the store.

Secondly, the information has to be processed. This processing takes place in the heart of the computer, the CPU, or central processing unit.

Lastly, the results of the processing have to be extracted, or output.

The complete computer configuration might be presented diagramatically, therefore, as shown below:

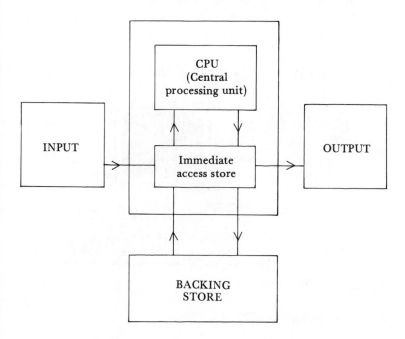

A *mainframe* computer is a large computer which is required to run a number of different processing tasks at the same time. *Minicomputers* are more compact, 'desk' size, lower priced computers, which nevertheless offer a high degree of versatility. *Microcomputers* are small, low cost computers built around the silicon chip *microprocessor*. The integrated circuits of these microprocessors are becoming smaller and smaller (the smallest can pass through the eye of a needle!). Progress is tremendously fast and as circuits become smaller, processing speed is becoming quicker, reliability is improving, and costs are coming down.

But, whatever the type or size of computer, the basic configuration remains the same.

A typical microcomputer system is depicted below. As can be seen the input is, in this case, via a keyboard and the output via the screen of a visual display unit. Alternatively, output in hard copy can be obtained from the printer. The backing or secondary storage is on disc. If instructions or data are input, via the keyboard, into the internal, 'immediate access' memory of the computer, this cannot remain there permanently. If it needs to be retained, or 'saved,' then it must be output to a disc. If it then becomes necessary to feed the data, etc, from the disc back into the computer, the disc is used for input. The disc may therefore be used for

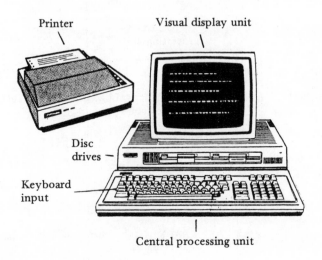

Printer

Visual display unit

Disc drives

Keyboard input

Central processing unit

Typical microcomputer system

output, for backing store, or for input. Cards or tapes (punched or magnetic) can perform different roles in the same way.

INPUT	SECONDARY STORAGE	OUTPUT
Keyboard		vdu
		Printer
Disc	Disc	Disc
Tape	Tape	Tape
Card	Card	Card

The above list is far from exhaustive. The reader may be aware, for instance, of the bar-code labels which can be 'read' by a light pen. These are used in some library circulation systems for the input of numbers representing books or readers. Some methods, eg optical character recognition, allow printed text to be 'read' for input and, ultimately, one will be able to 'talk' to the computer using a 'voice-activated' system.

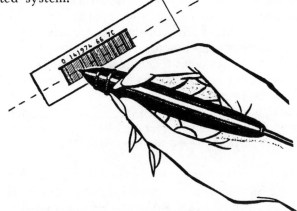

Reading the number from a bar-coded label by means of a light pen

What does it cost?

One could pay anything from under £50 to £500,000 or much more for a computer. The cheapest microcomputer uses a domestic television for output and a normal domestic cassette recorder to store instructions and data semi-permanently. A simple printer may be available for a further £40 or thereabouts.

Slightly up market, and into the range of microcomputers which are the smallest and cheapest which might realistically be used for business applications, there is, for example, the Commodore 64. At the time of writing this costs a mere £199. Peripheral costs are: cassette unit £45; disc drive £299; 14 inch colour monitor £230; printer £230; a complete system for under £1,000.

The Apple II was the microcomputer that really started a boom in the purchase of small computers for business purposes. Presently, another very popular microcomputer is the IBM Personal, which would cost about £3,000 for a system comprising computer, vdu and twin 'floppy' disc drives. A 'hard' disc system offering vastly increased storage capacity would cost a further £3,000.

The figures quoted here are given merely as a rough indication of prices. It should once again be noted that costs are continually falling, sometimes very sharply, and those shown above may now vary.[1]

Computers such as the IBM Personal have taken us into a new, fourth generation of microcomputers. This is the 16 bit as opposed to the 8 bit machine. As we have seen, 8 bits comprise one byte, equivalent to one character. The operating system of an 8 bit computer addresses 8 bits or one byte at a time. The 16 bit system addresses 16 bits, theoretically two characters at a time. Essentially, the 16 bit computer means faster and more efficient software and access to more RAM memory. Some machines operate with two processors, 8 bit and 16 bit, so that they retain compatibility with 8 bit software.

A recent inexpensive introduction to the microcomputer scene, the Sinclair QL, uses a 32 bit processor (the Motorola 68008) and offers 128K RAM expandable to 640K. It has built-in 'microdrives' each offering 100K of storage and altogether costs an incredibly low £399 including a suite of four software packages.

The price of a computer increases not only in relation to the basic system but with regard to the additional peripheral equipment that may be required. For example, a micro-

1 Prices given in this work were quoted originally in both UK pounds and US dollars. However, the rapidly changing rate of exchange made this rather meaningless. At the time of going to press the current rate is 1.11 UK pounds to the US dollar

computer with a facility for access via multiple terminals (a terminal being a means of accessing a computer but without the computer's processing power) would obviously push the cost up considerably.

It is difficult to assess where the basic microcomputer price range finishes. However, periodicals such as *What micro* tend to concentrate on the below £5–6,000 bracket. Above this price lie the minicomputers which currently offer possibly the best answer for many library operations. Again costs vary tremendously and one might pay anything from £6,000 to £40,000 and upwards for a minicomputer based system but the cost of a mainframe is far in excess of this and beyond the purchasing power of an individual library. Access to a mainframe may be possible because one is available within the superordinate organization, whether this be a local authority, academic institution, industrial undertaking, or some other institution. Alternatively, use could be made of a bureau which will process data as required for an appropriate payment. Obviously, the main advantage of using a bureau is that there is a minimal capital outlay.

What do you get for your money?
Processing power is cheap but, conversely, other computer components are relatively more expensive. A 'moving key' keyboard is one example and a cheap microcomputer may not have this facility but will employ some less costly alternative such as a touch sensitive board.

Speed of operation is another factor to be considered. Generally speaking, the better and more expensive the computer, the faster the machine.

A small, cheap computer may have a restricted immediate access memory which will permit only very elementary work to be done. At one time the maximum internal access store of a microcomputer was 32K but now much larger memories are available. Not all of this storage capacity can be used for instructions and data, a certain amount is required by the computer's operational system. This amount will increase with demand. For example, when operating with colour and high resolution graphics, a microcomputer might possibly need 20K of storage. If the maximum is 32K this does not leave much for other purposes.

A backing store such as cassette tape might hold something

in the order of 200K characters per '30 minutes' of tape. A 'floppy' disc might hold anything from 100K to 500K characters or more. A difficulty with tape is 'serial' access, ie to find something on the tape, all of the tape preceding the required item must be run through before the item is reached. Discs provide 'direct' or 'random' access, the 'read/write' head can go straight to the data required. This is a great advantage.

'Hard' discs, developed for the small computer have put massive storage capacity at the disposal of the microcomputer user; 5 megabytes, ie 5 million bytes, 20 megabytes, or much more on a single disc.

Of course, discs on large mainframe computers have always been 'hard' metal discs, usually in disc 'packs' and with enormous capacities.

We have seen that the simplest computer system might have a keyboard for input, a vdu and a printer for output, and cassette or disc drive for backing store.

It is possible, with some small computers to access them from more than one terminal. Alternatively, a number of microcomputers can be linked together to form a network.

However, this is still a long way from the amazing power of a large mini or mainframe computer. A typical mainframe installation is shown in diagrammatic form on the facing page, with a large capacity CPU, varied input and output via keyboard, card, disc, tape, vdu and printers, an enormous amount of secondary storage, and a facility of access from many remote terminals.

One or two details relating to the approximate speed at which the peripherals operate may be of interest. Cards can be 'read' at speeds of about 1,500 cards per minute and line printers (so called because they print a line at a time) can print at speeds of well over 1,000 lines per minute. Although such speeds can seem fast, relatively speaking this is not so, and card readers and line printers are referred to as 'slow peripherals.' The reason for this can be gleaned when one considers that a magnetic tape drive might transfer data to and from the processor at 20,000 characters per second. Even this pales into insignificance against the magnetic disc drive which can transfer data at 200,000 characters per second, with the discs rotating at 2,400 rpm. Tape and disc drives are referred to as 'fast peripherals.'

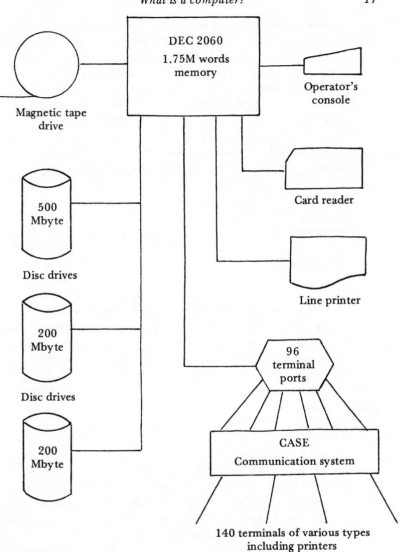

Illustrative mainframe computer installation. This is the DEC-20 system currently in use at Liverpool Polytechnic. M is an abbreviation for 'mega' or million

What equipment is required for a catalogue?

If the cataloguing agency has access to a mainframe or large minicomputer on a time sharing (see Glossary) basis then this is obviously to be preferred to a smaller system, *providing* the overall operational situation is satisfactory. There will be a need to ascertain the answers to such questions as:

1 Can the library system be kept up and running continually during the required periods?
2 Is the time taken by the computer to respond acceptable? This response time increases according to load.
3 If the system operates in batch (see Glossary) mode, are 'turn-around' times satisfactory?

If a computer has to be purchased, then the equipment will have to be selected in accordance with the money available. The chosen computer should, however:

1 Have sufficient immediate access memory. A suggested minimum for the microcomputer is 32/48K, although this is *very* small and could be completely inadequate for some purposes.
2 Be capable of handling the necessary peripherals such as disc drives, printer, etc. A printer and one or two floppy disc drives is the minimum practical requirement. Such a system has been used successfully in some institutions but, because of the restricted capacity of the floppy disc, the catalogue (unless the library stock were very small) would have to be stored on multiple discs, each containing a particular catalogue section.
3 Be capable of any expansion that might be necessary now, or that might become necessary in the future. Such expansion might include:
    i   Enhancement of immediate access store capacity, eg from 48K to 128K.
    ii Access from multiple terminals, ie expansion from a 'single user' system to one which can cope simultaneously with a number of users.
    iii Use of the computer as a means of communicating with other computers, ie as a terminal but a terminal which has the added advantage of built in processing power, or as one component of a computer network.
    iv Improvement in vdu definition, eg 40 character width to 80 character width.

A 16 bit (or higher) machine is probably the best microcomputer choice because it will usually contain more RAM which effectively reduces the number of times that the system has to access back up discs. This in turn means that the retrieval of information is faster.

A hard disc system is also essential when there is a large amount of data which has to be accessed quickly.

The minicomputer is a frequent choice for cataloguing operations as it offers much of the power and capability of the mainframe at a more reasonable price. It can support numerous peripherals and provide multi-user online access and it has the advantage of not requiring a special environment or a team of people to operate it.

Hardware and software

So far we have been discussing the actual equipment, or 'hardware,' that makes up a computer system. This hardware is, however, useless, unless it is given step by step instructions for performing specific operations. Such instructions, or 'programs', which will usually be held on disc or tape although increasingly plug-in ROM chips are also being used), together with any accompanying explanatory documentation, are referred to as 'software'.

Care should be taken, when buying a computer system, that appropriate software, ie suitable for the particular cataloguing requirement of the purchasing institution, is available, especially if there is no 'in-house' programming expertise. Many programs are specific *to* the particular machine, eg Apple II, or to the computer operating system, eg CP/M (a common system used in microcomputers with a Z80 microprocessor). Programs may also be language specific (eg PASCAL) and if the computer has another 'resident' programming language (usually BASIC on a small computer), extra circuitry may be required to adapt it, if, indeed, this is possible.

Apart from software developed in-house, other sources are:
a commercial suppliers, of which there are many
b other institutions using compatible equipment for similar purposes.

Where (b) is concerned, this might involve joining a co-operative scheme.

Software will be considered further in a later section.

Word processors

A word processor is simply a computer which is dedicated to the manipulation of textual matter. This includes the input, editing, formatting, storing and output of text. It is intended to improve · productivity by avoiding the need to retype material which has already been set up correctly.

If one wishes to change a particular word, sentence, paragraph, etc in a textual letter, report, article or whatever, which is stored in the machine, then the first priority is to locate that word, sentence, or paragraph. Thus a search facility is necessary.

As a catalogue is a series of textual records which is continually being updated and which continually needs to be searched for particular information, then it follows that a word processor could possibly be used for cataloguing purposes and certain libraries have, in fact, done this.

Some word processors also include a sort option which is a further cataloguing requirement.

However, although the dedicated word processor had, at one time, certain advantages over the microcomputer with a word processing package, the latter has improved enormously and the current trend seems to indicate a preference for the more flexible, non-dedicated system.

Online and offline

If one is communicating directly with the central processing unit of a computer then this is referred to as *online* access. An immediate response is obtained to messages and instructions. The opposite to online is *offline*, operating *without* direct and continuous communication with the main computer system.

For example, if cataloguing input is entered directly using a keyboard, whether this be in a stand-alone situation such as with a microcomputer or remotely via a terminal, then this is *online* operation. If a cataloguing form is completed manually and then sent off for punched cards or some other machine-readable format to be prepared for eventual input to the computer then this is *offline* operation. Offline is related to *batch processing,* ie jobs held back until there are sufficient to process in a group or batch.

When communication is online, the input and output devices can be physically separated from the central processor but connected to it by a land line or through the normal telecommunications network. The link between the latter and the terminal may be via a dedicated line or by means of a telephone. The telephone may be used to dial up the main computer and the terminal is then linked to the computer system via a *modem* or an *acoustic coupler*. The signal transmitted over the line is converted into a form suitable for the terminal and vice versa. 'Modem' is a contraction of modulator-demodulator. Unlike the modem, the acoustic coupler does not require an electrical connection. The handset simply fits into two rubber cups on the coupler.

With terminal access, the computer may be in the next room, the next building, the next city or even further away. Communication of this nature can be world wide and it is quite easy, with today's sophisticated communications network by satellite, etc, to sit at a terminal in one country and access a computer in another.

Remote online access, however, can be expensive in terms of (a) connect time charges for access to the host computer and (b) telecommunication costs. The greater the amount of in-house stand-alone processing that can be done the better. From this point of view, it can be advantageous to adapt a microcomputer so that it can also be used as a terminal. Data can then be captured online from the host and downloaded into the microcomputer's backing store for local processing. The use of the IBM Personal and Sirius microcomputers in this way for cataloguing purposes will be referred to later in this text.

Chapter Three

Files, records and fields

Information input to a computer is referred to as 'data'. Data may be organized into 'files' and a 'database' consists of one or more files. A file will contain a number of similar 'records' and each record is made up of elements called 'fields'.

A 'file' might, for example, be a library catalogue. Each individual entry in the catalogue is a 'record' and each element of the entry, eg ISBN, author, title, date, etc, is a 'field'.

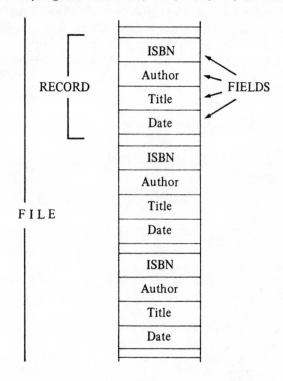

Fixed and variable fields

Fields may be in 'fixed' or 'variable' format. A fixed field is one of specific length in terms of characters (a character being a single letter, digit, punctuation mark, symbol or space). With fixed fields the computer is able to calculate which field it is handling at a given time by a count of characters from the beginning of the record. Elements which contain more than the specified number of characters must be truncated to fit the field length. Elements which contain less than the specified number of characters must be made up to the correct number by the addition of spaces. The title field in a catalogue record could, for example, be fixed at 20 characters. Examine the following titles of two of Shakespeare's plays:

    ROMEO AND JULIET
    MUCH ADO ABOUT NOTHING

The first title contains 16 characters (spaces *must* be counted) and the second 22 characters. To fit the fixed field length, *Romeo and Juliet* must have four characters, ie spaces, added and *Much ado about nothing* must lose 2 characters, eg:

R	O	M	E	O		A	N	D		J	U	L	I	E	T				

M	U	C	H		A	D	O		A	B	O	U	T		N	O	T	H	I

Fixed fields are reasonably simple to manipulate by computer but they do pose certain problems. For example, the truncation of the latter title could obviously be achieved in a number of different ways, eg:

M	U	C	H		A		A	B	O	U	T		N	O	T	H	I	N	G

M	U	C	H		A	D	O		A	B	T		N	O	T	H	I	N	G

etc.

How is consistency to be achieved? Is the title still recognizable and understandable? Will searching be affected? These are just a few of the questions which must be asked.

With variable fields, each field may contain a varying number of characters. The length of records and constituent fields will now differ. The beginning and end of each record and each field must therefore be marked by identification 'tags' which the computer can recognize.

The first title used as an example above, for instance,

might be tagged with a £T to indicate the beginning of the title and a hash mark (#) to indicate its end, eg:

£ T R O M E O   A N D   J U L I E T #

The characters used as tags must be unique and used for this purpose only. They must not occur elsewhere in the record. An alternative to the special symbol indicating the end of each variable field is a 'record and field length count' field, included at the beginning of the record.

Variable fields offer obvious advantages but they are more difficult to manipulate and to search.

It should be noted that even if variable length format *is* used, certain fields, eg accession number, may still be of fixed length. The record will therefore consist of a mixture of fixed and variable length fields.

Whether the format is fixed or variable, it must be stressed that all of the records in a file must have a similar format, with elements cited in a consistent order, although a particular element, eg a series, may not be present in every record.

Key field

One field may have a higher status than other fields and is therefore called the *key* field because, when searching for a particular record within a file, it would normally be this field which would act as a unique identifier. The key field will usually be the first. The ISBN or International Standard Book Number (see Glossary) could be utilized for this purpose. Alternatively, an in-house running number could be generated. In this latter instance, numbers can be made 'meaningful' to the cataloguing agency. For example, the first digit could indicate whether the item is fiction, non-fiction, audio-visual material, etc; other digits could indicate the library or branch to which the item is allocated, whilst the remaining digits would comprise a unique identifier.

The key field could, of course, be something other than a number, eg the author. More than one field might also comprise the key, either concatenated or used separately.

Record organization

The manner in which a record is organized will depend upon the requirements of the individual cataloguing agency. A reasonably short, fixed field might well be suitable for some library systems, as such records are easier and quicker to

Author — Surname

| H | A | Y | N | E | S | | | | | | |

Author — Forname

| C | O | N | N | I | E |

Title

| S | P | E | E | D | , | | S | T | R | E | N | G | T | H |
| A | N | D | | S | T | A | M | I | N | A | | | | |

Catalogue record in 'fixed' field format. Author's surname limited to maximum of twelve characters; forename to maximum of six characters; title to maximum of thirty characters in this particular example

100 $A HAYNES $H CONNIE #

245 $A SPEED, STRENGTH AND STAMINA
$B CONDITIONING FOR TENNIS #

Catalogue record in 'variable' field format. Each element is 'tagged' for identification. Here tag 100 identifies the author field; $A is a subfield code for the author's surname and $H the forename. Tag 245 identifies the title field; $A is the subfield code for the title proper and $B the subtitle. Such tags, codes and other indicators are used in the MARC format, which is to be discussed on the following pages

compile and to search and they do provide a workable 'finding list' type catalogue. A fixed field input form used by Sefton Libraries (UK) is reproduced on page 27. Here the author field is limited to 24 characters and the title field to

48 characters. On the other hand, a national library, with a commitment to the provision of a sophisticated bibliographic service, would find such a fixed format unacceptable because elements of bibliographic data are of widely differing and unpredictable lengths. Here, for example, are two further book titles:

CATALOGUING

OUT OF THE DINOSAURS : THE EVOLUTION OF
THE NATIONAL LENDING LIBRARY FOR
SCIENCE AND TECHNOLOGY

The first title is 10 characters in length and the second 95 characters in length. With a fixed field format, a field length of about 100 characters would be required to accommodate the latter. This would be extremely wasteful for the shorter title because 90 'spaces' would have to be stored. A fixed field length of 20 characters would be ample for this first title but the second work would then lose its very informative sub-title, leaving only a misleading title proper. A compromise length of 50 characters would again be wasteful for the first title and would cause problems in relation to truncation with the second.

The saving in storage space when variable length fields are used can be considerable. If, for example, the maximum size which has to be allowed for in a catalogue record is 500 characters (or bytes) and the average size of a record is only 250 characters, then the saving, if variable length as against fixed length fields were used, would be 250 × the number of records. In a catalogue of say 10,000 items, this would be 10,000 × 250 bytes!

Sample record format
A simple, sample record format adopted by a library might consist of eight fields, viz ISBN, Title, Responsible person or body, Edition, Publisher, Date, Classification number and Subject. Each field could be fixed at the following respective lengths in characters: ISBN — 10; Title — 66; Responsibility — 40; Edition — 10; Publisher — 20; Date — 4; Class no — 10 (this would allow classification to six or seven decimal places if the scheme in use were the Dewey Decimal Classification) and Subject — 40. The total length of the record would be 200 characters.

Fixed field input form used at Sefton Libraries. Author field limited to 24 characters. Short title field limited to 48 characters. Actual size 13 × 8 in

The format is shown below with sample data entered for two different items. Some standard conventions are used to illustrate how the task of the operator who inputs the data can be made easier. The 'I' is 'top and tailed' to distinguish it from a '1' and the digit ∅ and the letter $ are 'crossed' to distinguish them from the letter O and the digit 5.

The detail supplied for the two items is very much the same and they would appear to be catalogued quite correctly. However, the information relating to the second item might

ISBN

| ∅ | 9 | ∅ | ∅ | 8 | 4 | I | ∅ | 2 | 8 |

TITLE

| H | O | M | E | | B | R | E | W | E | D | | B | E | E | R | $ | | A | N | D | |

| $ | T | O | U | T | $ | | | | | | | | | | | | | | | | |

| | | | | | | | | | | | | | | | | | | | | | |

RESPONSIBILITY

| B | E | R | R | Y | | C | | J | | J | | | | | | | | |

| | | | | | | | | | | | | | | | | | | |

EDITION

| 4 | T | H | | E | D | | | |

PUBLISHER

| A | M | A | T | E | U | R | | W | I | N | E | M | A | K | E | R | | |

DATE   **CLASS**

| I | 9 | 7 | ∅ | | 6 | 4 | I | · | 8 | 7 | 3 | | |

SUBJECT

| B | E | E | R | | | | | | | | | | | | | | | | |

| | | | | | | | | | | | | | | | | | | | |

Sample record format — example 1

well be considered inadequate. The work has, in fact, been
revised and enlarged by Ingvald Marm and, in addition, it is
one of the *Teach yourself series.*

A number of difficulties may be encountered when such a
format is used. Select some items at random from your home
or library book shelves and examine the problems that could
occur if they were catalogued accordingly.

A useful exercise would be to design a new format which
would attempt to cater for the problems that are encountered.

ISBN

| 0 | 3 | 4 | 0 | 0 | 5 | 8 | 0 | 9 | 9 |

TITLE

| N | O | R | W | E | G | I | A | N | | : | | A | | B | O | O | K | | O | F | |

| S | E | L | F | - | I | N | S | T | R | U | C | T | I | O | N | | I | N | | T | H |

| E | | N | O | R | W | E | G | I | A | N | | R | I | K | S | M | A | L | | | |

RESPONSIBILITY

| S | O | M | M | E | R | F | E | L | T | | A | L | F | | | | | | |

| | | | | | | | | | | | | | | | | | | | | |

EDITION

| N | E | W | | E | D | | | | |

PUBLISHER

| H | O | D | D | E | R | | A | N | D | | S | T | O | U | G | H | T | O | N |

DATE   CLASS

| 1 | 9 | 6 | 7 | | 4 | 3 | 9 | . | 8 | 2 | | | |

SUBJECT

| N | O | R | W | E | G | I | A | N | | L | A | N | G | U | A | G | E | | |

| | | | | | | | | | | | | | | | | | | | | | | | |

Sample record format — example 2

Whilst doing this, however, it should be borne in mind that many libraries and, indeed, many users, find a short entry perfectly satisfactory (see also page 194). A full entry continues to be used, of course, in, for example, national bibliographies.

Standardization

A library which acted unilaterally and designed an in-house record format such as that just described would encounter a further problem. It would be unable to exchange bibliographic data with other institutions, as the record formats would be incompatible.

A clear distinction must therefore be made between a local, or in-house, format and a communication, or exchange, format. An in-house format is primarily concerned with efficient and cost-effective computer processing for the particular institution concerned. The exchange format's main objective is to provide a record structure which is hospitable to the needs and requirements of a wide variety of systems. In order to achieve this objective, the organization of the record must be standardized.

There are three things to be considered:[1]

1 The basic structure or framework of the record
2 The field names (sometimes called designators, labels, or attributes)
3 The record contents or data.

Some degree of standardization can be applied to all three of these. With regard to (1) and (2) the best known record format is the MARC (MAchine Readable Cataloguing) format. MARC conforms to *Anglo-American cataloguing rules*, 2nd edition, (AACR2). In the English speaking world and in some other countries, eg Norway, the latter is the major current standard for the description of a bibliographic item and for selecting and formulating the access points through which the item may be retrieved. AACR2 is, therefore, apart from certain aspects of the subject approach, also important in relation to (3).

1 *Compatibility issues affecting information systems and services* / prepared by F. Wilfrid Lancaster and Linda C. Smith for the General Information Programme and UNISIST. — Unesco, 1983

MARC format

The MARC format is a variable length field format and each element must therefore be tagged for identification. As noted above, MARC conforms to AACR2 and the description of an item formulated according to these rules would contain the following areas:

Title and statement of responsibility
Edition
Material (or type of publication) specific details
Publication, distribution, etc
Physical description
Series
Note(s)
Standard number and terms of availability

The MARC tag for the title and statement of responsibility area, for example, is 245. This is followed by an indicator which provides the machine with certain other information and then subfield codes to identify the various elements within the area.

Here is a title and statement of responsibility tagged according to MARC:

245   10 $aBorn free$ba lioness of two worlds$dby Joy Adamson#

The tag 245 is followed by the digits 1 which indicates that a title entry will be required (otherwise 0) and 0 which indicates that no characters are to be ignored when filing (otherwise 2, 3, or 4 if the title began with an indefinite or definite article). The $a is the subfield code for the title proper, the $b is the subfield code for other title information, a subtitle in this instance, and the $d is the subfield code for a simple, single author statement of responsibility. The field is terminated with a hash mark (#).

The heading for the main access point (usually the responsible person or body) would be tagged with a number beginning with 1. 100 is the tag for a person as main entry heading and the indicator 10 reveals that this is a person with a single surname. $a is the subfield code for the entry element and $h for other parts of the name, ie:

100 10 $aAdamson$hJoy#

The tag for the publication area is 260. The digits 00

indicate that the publisher is not the main entry heading. The subfield codes are $a for place, $b for publisher, and $c for date, ie:

260 00 $aLondon$bCollins$c1960#

Three areas of the entry have now been tagged and indentified:

100 10 $aAdamson$hJoy#
245 10$aBorn free$ba lioness of two worlds$d by Joy Adamson#
260 00 $aLondon$bCollins$c1960#

Other areas would be tagged and identified in a similar fashion to complete a full MARC record.

On pages 34 and 35 will be found a reproduction of an illustrative and shortened version of a MARC input form, with an abbreviated schedule of field tags, indicators and subfield codes, as used for teaching purposes at Liverpool Polytechnic. The form is shown completed with details relating to a sample item.

Part of an actual British Library MARC input form is reproduced on the facing page.

Evolution of MARC

MARC came into being in the United States in 1966 with a pilot project which involved the weekly distribution of machine-readable tapes to sixteen selected libraries. These libraries processed the tapes through their own computing facilities, the most common requirement being, at that time, the production of catalogue cards!

A more advanced version of the scheme, using what became known as the MARC II format, became operational in 1967 with, initially, about fifty libraries receiving tapes on a subscription basis. In that same year, the British National Bibliography began work upon the development of a MARC system in the UK and tapes were being distributed to libraries by 1969.

MARC I had certain limitations; MARC II made the record format much more flexible. Variable length fields are used and each record is capable of holding a vast amount of information (up to 6,000 characters in the UK format, although

	Item number

BL CATALOGUING INPUT – MONOGRAPHS

ISBN				BNB Issue No.		
001	#	#		039	$p	$a

Uniform Title	
240	
243	

Title	
245	
245.1	
245.3	

Part title	
248	

Edition	
250	

Imprint	
260	
260.1	

Physical description							
	$b	ill	$i		chart		map
					coat of arms		music
300	$c	cm			facsim		plan
					form		port
	$e	pbk	cased	spiral	unbound	geneal table	sample

Linking ISBN		BNB Serial no.	
021		015	

Language		LC card no.	
041		010	

Price		Receipt date	
350		957	c#

Notes	
5XX	

Information codes								
008	$a	$b	$c	$d	$e	$f	$g	$h
	$i	$j	$	$l	$m	$o	$p W	

BSD PC4 2

Cataloguing input form used by the Bibliographic Services Division of the British Library

Liverpool Polytechnic
School of Librarianship and Information Studies

MARC FORMAT CATALOGUING SHEET

ISBN 021	021 00 $a 0340058099 #
Accession number 029	029 00 $a 17643 #
Personal author or responsible body 100	100 10 $a Sommerfelt $h Alf #
Uniform title 240	
Title 245	245 10 $a Norwegian $b a book of self-instruction in the Norwegian Riksmal $d Alf Sommerfelt #
Edition 250	250 00 $a New ed. $c completely rev. and enlarged by Ingvald Marm #
Publication details 260	260 00 $a London $b Hodder and Stoughton $c 1967 #
Physical description 300	300 00 $a xiv, 281 p. $c 18 cm #
Series 400	440 00 $a Teach yourself books #
Library's holdings 998	998 00 $a 01 : HOI #

MARC input form used for teaching purposes at Liverpool Polytechnic, completed in accordance with the abbreviated statement of field tags, indicator and subfield definitions shown opposite

SCHEDULES

Tag	Indicator	Subfield code	Definition
021	00	$a	ISBN
029	00	$a	Accession number
100	10		Person entered under single surname
		$a	Entry element
		$e	Additions to names, e.g. Sir, Dame
		$h	Forenames
	20		Compound surnames
		$a	Entry element
		$e	Additions to names
		$h	Parts of the name other than the entry element
110			Corporate headings
	10		Government bodies
		$a	Entry element
		$c	Subordinate agencies — repeated when necessary
	20		Corporate bodies other than govts. and confs.
		$a	Entry element
		$c	Subordinate headings — repeated when necessary
111	00		Conference headings
		$a	Entry element
		$i	Number
		$j	Location
		$k	Date
240	10	$a	Uniform title
245	0		No title entry required
	1		Title entry required
	3		Title proper is main entry heading

Second indicator 0—9 = number of characters to be ignored in filing

		Subfield	
		$a	Title proper
		$b	Other title information
		$d	Statement of responsibility — simple, single author
		$e	Statement of responsibility differing from, or adding to, info. in $d, e.g. 'edited by', etc.
250	00	$a	Edition statement
		$c	Statement of responsibility relating to edition
260	00		Publisher not main entry heading
	10		Publisher main entry heading
		$a	Place
		$b	Publisher
		$c	Date
300	00	$a	Pagination
		$b	Illustration
		$c	Size
440	00	$a	Series title
		$v	Number
998	00	$a	Library's holdings note, e.g. 01:H01, i.e. 'One copy in Humanities Library'

EJH/Jan. 1984

On this input form, the information to the left of the vertical line refers the cataloguer to the schedules given above. Cataloguing data is to be written in the boxes to the right of the vertical line, together with the appropriate tags, indicators and subfield codes. Each field must be marked at the end by a 'field terminator', ie #.

It should be noted that in the MARC format tags ending in '9' and tags 950-998 are reserved for local needs.

the average is 1,000 characters)[1] and a considerable number of elements. Apart from all of the information which would be found in a full description by AACR2, there are many additional fields, eg Dewey decimal and Library of Congress classification numbers, Library of Congress subject headings, PRECIS subject index entries, etc. Any of these elements may be used as a means of approach. In addition, provision is made for information of 'local' significance to be included, for example a library 'holdings' note.

The MARC format caters (as does AACR2) for a variety of library materials, monographs, serials, music, etc. The system is no longer confined to Britain and America. Many countries, including Australia, Canada, France, Germany, Netherlands, Japan, Scandinavia and South Africa have agreed to work to the same MARC format standard.

MARC now spreads its influence across the whole spectrum of library activity; including selection, ordering, cataloguing, information retrieval, production of bibliographies, etc. MARC can now be accessed online and the system is at the heart of many library networks.

Structure of MARC

The structure of the UK MARC record may be shown diagrammatically thus:

SEGMENT CONTROL WORD	RECORD LABEL	DIREC- TORY	CONTROL FIELDS	VARIABLE DATA FIELDS	

The *segment control word* is a machine requirement for the processing of the records. The *label* contains information relating to the record such as its length, its status, eg new record, and its type and class, eg printed monograph. The *directory* is a guide to the content of the record, listing each tag, the number of characters in the particular field, and the starting character position within the record.

Following the directory are the *control fields* which contain information such as the ISBN, date of entry on the file, date of publication, language of the text, country of publication, etc.

Lastly comes the actual bibliographic *data* contained in variable length fields. This includes: a full bibliographical description, together with headings, or access points, as required by AACR2; a set of subject data; and other supplementary information.

Although the structure shown here is that of the UK MARC format, all such formats will usually consist of the three major elements: a leader providing general information about the record; a directory which is a guide to the content; and the data itself.

The MARC format is undoubtedly the world's most important bibliographic record format and certain other standards, eg the international standard ISO 2709–1981, *Format for bibliographic information interchange on magnetic tape*, have derived from it.

Anglo-American cataloguing rules. 2nd edition. (AACR2). 1978

As noted on page 30, MARC conforms to AACR2 and it is therefore divided into specified areas, always cited in the same order. Within each area, AACR2 provides guidance on the elements to be included, for example the publication, distribution, etc area might include place of publication, publisher and date; the order in which these elements are to be cited will also be specified.

The rules for description in AACR2 are based upon the framework of ISBD(G) — International Standard Bibliographic Description (General) — which was drawn up jointly by the Joint Steering Committee for AACR and the IFLA International Office for UBC (IFLA = International Federation of Library Associations and institutions; UBC = Universal Bibliographic Control). IFLA has produced a number of additional standards for specific materials, eg ISBD(S) for serials, ISBD(NBM) for non-book materials, etc, all adhering to the general framework.

There is, however, a major difference between *cataloguing* rules and rules for *bibliographic description*. The latter, as the term implies, concerns itself only with describing an item. A full set of cataloguing rules such as AACR2 concerns

SCW	Record label													Directory			
0	0744	00739	n	a	m	ƀƀ	2	2	00277	ƀ	ƀƀ	4	5	ƀƀ	001 0011 00000	008 0041 00011	010 0014 00052

015 0013 00066	050 0010 00079	081 0014 00089	082 0014 00103	083 0018 00117	100 0020 00135

245 0050 00155	260 0043 00205	300 0023 00248	350 0010 00271	440 0042 00281	500 0052 00323

504 0010 00375	650 0018 00385	690 0025 00403	691 0012 00428	692 0012 00440	790 0009 00452#

Control No.	Information codes												LC Card No.
0060426780#	720329	s1971ƀƀƀƀ	enƀ	aƀƀƀ	ƀ	W	ƀƀƀƀ	00011	ƀ	ƀ	eng	ƀƀ#	00 \$a74-141171#

BNB No.	LC Class No.	Old DC No.	Current DC No.	Feature	
00 \$aB7208387#	00 \$aQA273#	00 \$a519.2\$c18#	00 \$a519.2\$c19#	00 \$aProbabilities#	

Heading		Title	
10 \$aHausner\$hMelvin#		10 \$aElementaryƀprobabilityƀtheory\$dMelvinƀHausner#	

Imprint		Collation		Price	
00 \$aNewƀYork\$aLondon\$bHarperƀandƀRow\$c1971#		00 \$aix,310p\$bill\$c25cm#		00 \$a£4.15#	

Series statement		Note	
00 \$aHarper'sƀseriesƀinƀmodernƀmathematics#		00 \$aWithƀanswersƀtoƀselectedƀ	

		Note	Subject heading	PRECIS string	
odd-numberedƀexercises#		00 \$aIndex#	00 \$aProbabilities#	00 \$z21030\$aprobabilities#	

SIN		RIN		Tracing		
00 \$a0000272#		00 \$a0000663#		00 \$a1.Tﬤ#	*	

Example of a MARC record stored on magnetic tape

itself not only with description but also with the choice and form of access points, or headings, under which an item may be filed or identified. More will be said about this point under 'input of data' in the next chapter.

UNIMARC

Although the overall format structure of MARC remained the same in whichever country that it was adopted, the content designators (tags, indicators, etc) varied greatly in the different national formats because of certain continuing differences in cataloguing practice. Thus one national agency wishing to process the MARC data of another national agency had to write a special computer program to do so and separate programs would be needed for every such format that the agency wished to make use of meaning costly *multiple* conversion programs.

This led to the development of UNIMARC. It was not possible to design one format that would meet equally the requirements of all MARC users but UNIMARC is intended to be a *communication* format, which would make it necessary to write and maintain only *two* conversion programs — one from the national format to UNIMARC and one from UNIMARC to the national format. UNIMARC standardizes content designators for a core element, a 'descriptive block,' which is based on the ISBD. A second edition of UNIMARC was published by the IFLA International Office for UBC in 1980.

A basic principle of UBC (Universal Bibliographic Control) is that national agencies who so desire may take advantage of cataloguing work being carried out in the country in which a particular item originated.[1] UNIMARC could make a significant contribution to UBC but, if it is to succeed, it requires the co-operation and effort, not to mention the financial outlay, of all national MARC users. A number of national agencies have already expressed a commitment and the Library of Congress has completed specifications to convert its MARC records to UNIMARC format.

As yet, however, there is still very little international

1 UNIMARC / Henriette D. Avram and Sally H. McCallum *IFLA journal* 8 (1982) 1 50-54

exchange of bibliographic data and what there is does not involve the use of UNIMARC.[1]

A test commissioned by the International MARC Network Study Steering Committee and undertaken at the Deutsche Bibliothek has indicated some weaknesses in UNIMARC when compared with other international exchange formats, in particular the UNISIST *Reference manual* (see following pages). It was therefore proposed that an interpretive handbook be prepared which would clarify some of the areas of uncertainty. This handbook was published in 1983 (*UNIMARC handbook* / compiled and edited by A. Hopkinson with S. McCallum and S.P. Davis. IFLA International Office for UBC).

Reference manual for machine-readable bibliographic descriptions

For some years development and testing has been proceeding on an international *Reference manual for machine-readable bibliographic descriptions* and a second revised edition of this *Manual* was published by UNESCO in 1981. The work was begun within the framework of UNISIST, a project to study the feasibility of a world science and technology information network. Whilst the *Manual* was conceived for use by abstracting and indexing services, it was hoped that it would have other applications in the wider field of information processing and exchange. The second edition therefore includes, for instance, guidelines for the description of serials and monographs in their own right.

The major objective of the *Manual* is to serve as a standardized communication format for the exchange of machine-readable bibliographic information. However, it can also be used by non-computerized systems. Although the *Manual* contains all the elements necessary for cataloguing, it stops short of formulating any precise cataloguing rules. It is concerned only with rules for bibliographic description.

Examples of tags used in the *Manual* are A09 Title of monograph; A12 Person associated with monograph; A18

1 International access to bibliographic data : MARC and MARC-related activities / Alan Hopkinson *Journal of documentation* 40 (1) March 1984 13-24

Corporate body associated with monograph; A25 Publisher's name and location. As with MARC, indicator and subfield codes are also used.

Common communication format

Work continues on a proposed common communication format which would serve the purposes of libraries, documentation centres, abstracting and indexing publications, and information services of all types. This is being developed by a UNESCO ad hoc group and since UNIMARC and the *Reference manual* . . . are major source formats, it is to be expected that the CCF will be compatible with both.

Not everyone is agreed that such a format is attainable (or even desirable) but certain principles have already been identified as a basis for development. The structure should conform to ISO 2709 and standards and/or standard techniques should be applied to the core bibliographic description, any additional descriptive elements, and the data elements (eg classification number).

Chapter Four

Input and storage of data

Input of data
Records may be entered 'offline' or 'online.' Where the former is concerned, an input form such as those shown on pages 27, 28 and 33 is normally completed by the cataloguer and this is then passed on for 'translation' into machine-readable form, eg punched cards, for inputting to the computer.

With an online system, records are input to the computer *direct* via a keyboard. 'Prompts' may appear, in some form, on the screen of the visual display unit, eg

```
ENTER ISBN
?
```

```
ENTER ISBN
?  0 13 093963 3
ENTER AUTHOR
?
```

```
ENTER ISBN
?  0 13 093963 3
ENTER AUTHOR
?  CLIFTON, H.D.
ENTER TITLE
?
```

```
ENTER ISBN
?  0 13 093963 3
ENTER AUTHOR
?  CLIFTON, H.D.
ENTER TITLE
?  BUSINESS DATA SYSTEMS
```

When entering data online using a MARC based system, the prompts may comprise the appropriate MARC tags, eg ENTER 100 (for author), ENTER 245 (for title), etc. The cataloguer or operator who enters the data will need to know something of the MARC structure, especially as subfield codes and other relevant detail may have to be included in the input. The BLAISE (British Library Automated Information SErvice) EDITOR system is one example of a service currently using this methodology but the British Library is apparently intending to replace it in the not too distant future with something which is a little more user-friendly.

In the examples given above, the particular field content must be entered before the next prompt appears. The prompts could, however, appear all at once in a complete screen format, eg:

```
ISBN: ..........
TITLE: ...................................................................
RESPONSIBILITY:...........................................
EDITION:..........
PUBLISHER:....................
DATE: ....          CLASS:..........
SUBJECT: .........................................
```

In this instance, the number of full stops, or periods, could indicate field lengths. An examination of the above format will reveal that it is similar to that of the input form shown on page 27. In some 'form-filling' online systems, the 'form', ie the screen format, can be tailored to meet specific user requirements. One such system is DEMAND, which interfaces with the 1022 database package on the DEC-20 mainframe. This is used in Liverpool Polytechnic Library for a special catalogue of videotapes. The format is shown overleaf.

(Some of the fields, eg Log number, are required under licencing arrangements for the recording of tapes such as Open University television programmes). Field lengths are indicated as explained above and the cursor (see Glossary) can be made to 'jump' from field to field for entry or amendment.

```
SEQUENCE: ...............
POSITION: .
LOCATION:...................
TITLE: ..........................................
        ................................
DISTRIBUTOR: .....................
PRODUCER: ...................................
LENGTH:...
LOG_NUMBER: ...
KW: ..........................................
     ................................
NOTE:.........................................
     ................................
```

The use of the cursor as described above is a convenient and often used editing facility. Other possibilities are commands such as DELETE or CHANGE followed by an indication of the field(s) or data to be amended, eg:

CHANGE AUTHOR SMYTHE

which means change the author field to 'Smythe', and function keys for activities such as the removal of complete lines. In menu-driven systems, options will be included in the choices displayed on the screen, eg:

1 ADD RECORD
2 AMEND RECORD
3 DELETE RECORD
4 DISPLAY RECORD

Some systems make use of a combination of the various methods, eg menu and command mode, or menu and form-filling mode. Here, for instance, is the operator's menu from the microcomputer based LIBRARIAN system as used at the

University of Buckingham (UK)[1] (see also page 136). The operator mode, as distinct from the user mode, can only be entered by way of a password, so as to protect the data from unauthorized amendment.

```
Insert   .  .  .  .   I
Amend    .  .  .  .   A
Delete   .  .  .  .   D
List     .  .  .  .   L
Menu     .  .  .  .   M
```

If I is selected, a blank record appears on the screen:

```
Acc no : . . . . . . . .     ISBN : . . . . . . . . . .
Record :
. . . . . . . . . . . . . . . . . . . . . . . . . . . . . . . . . . . . . . . . . . . . . . . . .
. . . . . . . . . . . . . . . . . . . . . . . . . . . . . . . . . . . . . . . . . . . . . . . . .
Classification : . . . . . . . . . . . . .
Codes :  . . . . . . . .      . . . . . . . .      . . . . . . . .
         . . . . . . . .      . . . . . . . .      . . . . . . . .
Type :   . . . . . . . .
```

As each field is entered, the cursor jumps to the next field. Machine based checks are made, such as for the correct number of characters in the accession number or ISBN. The 'record' field consists of 156 characters and comprises author(s), title, edition, publisher, date of publication and call number. Author/title codes, of which there are up to six, are made up in different ways, eg the first four letters of the first two significant words for a responsible corporate body (LIVEPOLY = Liverpool Polytechnic). The 'type' field can be used for various codes such as SLC = Short Loan Collection.

It may, of course, be necessary, initially, for the cataloguer to search a data base in order to ascertain whether a record is already present. The operator must have ready access to the enquiry mode. In LIBRARIAN, searching may be achieved by ISBN, accession number, classification, type, or author/ title acronymic codes. These are typical access points.

1 Cataloguing on a micro with LIBRARIAN / John E. Pemberton *Library micromation news* (3) January 1984 7-14

In a command based system, searches will usually be entered by means of a command, followed by the appropriate field, followed by the search term or code, eg:

```
SEARCH NUMBER 0851573584
SEARCH AUTHOR HUNTER
SEARCH AUTHOR HUNT,ERI,J
SEARCH TITLE WAR,OF,TH,W
```

Commands and fields may be abbreviated:

```
s/n/0851573584
s/a/HUNTER
s/a/HUNT,ERI,J
s/t/WAR,OF,TH,W
```

Commands could also be made implicit and the search term or code entered directly:

```
HUNT,ERI,J
```

Searching is referred to here from the cataloguer's point of view and not the user's. Online searching will be discussed more fully at a later stage.

When a catalogue record is retrieved, it may not be one that the searching agency itself has generated. It could, in a centralized or co-operative system, be a national library supplied MARC record, or a record compiled by some other library. The searching agency must then decide whether it wishes to use this record, in whole or in part, as a basis for its own cataloguing.

A retrieved record will be displayed on the screen and any required amendments or additions can then be made to suit the individual library. Such amendments will be made as previously indicated, by cursor control, editing commands, and so on. Display formats can be complex, especially if MARC is used, and very careful checking will be necessary. There may also be a need for diagnostic print-outs for offline perusal.

If a record is not retrieved, the searching agency will then compile one and, if the agency belongs to a network, this record can then be made available to other participants.

Here, as one illustrative example, are some of the possible online transactions open to users of the MARC based shared cataloguing SWALCAP network (see also page 180). These have been reduced in number for ease of explanation.

ACQUIRE NEW RECORD
CREATE RECORD
AMEND RECORD
REQUEST PROOFSHEET
DELETE RECORD

The ACQUIRE NEW RECORD option is used for acquiring, online, for in-house use, new MARC records from within the network and for generating orders to outside suppliers for requests not satisfied within the system. Access to the million-plus records on the SWALCAP database is by control number or by one of several acronym keys based on the author, the title, or a combination of author and title. (Access by keyword is also possible in some circumstances).

Once acquired, a record is copied to the requester's file and is immediately available for online amendment.

The AMEND RECORD option displays a record on the screen in filtered format, ie without those fields which the user has specified in the processing parameters as not being of interest. All editing takes place at local level in a minicomputer. A series of editing commands, rather than cursor movement, are used to edit data. Examples are:

ERASE (delete subfield)
APPEND (add new subfield to the end of the field)
TRADE (alter each occurrence of one sequence of characters for another)
CHANGE (alter subfield as detailed)
INSERT (insert new subfield as detailed)

A field which needs alteration is indicated by the command SELECT and this field is then displayed on its own with each subfield starting on a new line and referenced by a line number, which helps to simplify the editing process.

When the CREATE RECORD option is selected, the user will input a control number, which is then verified by the system and, if acceptable, the computer sends to the terminal a 'dummy' as the basis for the new record. This dummy is expanded into a full catalogue record using the same technique as that used in the amendment or enlargement of a record. A line is chosen using the command SELECT (Line

No) and the command INSERT is used to enter data on that line.

The REQUEST PROOFSHEET option will enable a diagnostic hard copy print of a SWALCAP/MARC record to be obtained for checking purposes. It is very similar to the form in which the same MARC record would be displayed on a screen.

When using certain search techniques, eg acronymic keys, a number of different records may match the input. The SWALCAP system displays these in brief format and the operator can scan or 'page' through the matches until the required record is found. This may then be displayed in a fuller format using an EXPAND command.

Some systems incorporate a 'browse' mechanism, so that records immediately preceding or following a displayed record may be viewed.

```
>rimm,g??,?<


1.   Rimmington, G.T.  Education, politics and society in Leicester, 1833-1940
     1974.
     0123456789    User FRO(40)  Function m  Supplement File
     Also held by:  CDF(20) BET(56)

2.   Rimmington, G.T.  The Great Plague in Leicestershire, 1980.
     X401010101    User FRN(41)  Function m  Supplement File
   >>>RECORD HELD BY YOUR LIBRARY
     Also held by:  SWA(65) UWI(25)

3.   Rimmler, Gordon E.  Catalan for beginners. 1974.
     0011223344    User EXE(30)  Function m  Catalogue File

4.   Rimmington, Graham.  Education, politics and society in Leicester,
     1833-1940. 1974.
     0123456789    User REA(90)  Function m  Supplement File
```

Brief display of SWALCAP record (Acronym access)

Input methodology in computerized cataloguing will differ from system to system. Various combinations of online and offline operation are possible. For example, online access might be used for checking whether an item is already in the database and for record verification. A manual input form could then be prepared for any item not in the base and the detail present therein could subsequently be entered online by a keyboard operator. A library could also

TRANSACTION NAME   PAGE   1

CONTROL NO.   USER   AMENDED   FUNCTION   FILE
123456789   40   08-FEB-83   M   SUPPLEMENT (CATALOGUING)

1   008:0/0.00 $as1974 $ben $c $d $e $f $g0 $h0 $i0 $j0 $k0

                 $l $m $neng $o $p4 $qa $rm#

2   009:0/0.00 $ask $b0 $c0#

3   050:0/0.00 $aDN63.R6#

5   100:0/0.10 $aRimmington$hG.T#

6   245:0/0.10 . $aEducation, politics and society in Leicester, 1833-1940$eby

                 G.T. Rimmington and Jacques Grevin#
                                       A
7   260:0/0.00 $aLeicester$bLeicestershire Record Office$c1974#

8   300:0/0.00 $a151p#

9   350:0/0.00 $a 4.95#
                 P
12 700.0/0.00 $aGrevin$hJacques#
                 A
* CONTINUED

- - - - - - - - - - - - - end of page 1 -

TRANSACTION NAME   PAGE   2

CONTROL NO.   USER   AMENDED   FUNCTION   FILE
123456789   40   08-FEB-83   M   SUPPLEMENT (CATALOGUING)

13 960:0/0.00 A $a4000042733$eSigned copy$a4000530918#

14 962:0/0.20 A $a4000042771#

15 970:0/0.00 A $aHC123#

14 972:0/0.20 A $aDN63.R6#

Screen display of SWALCAP/MARC record

make use of online facilities to search and catalogue but
provide an offline public service, eg a microfiche catalogue.

Whatever the method of input, data will have to be checked
for accuracy. This may involve: (1) reading through completed input forms; (2) checking records online as they are
displayed on a vdu; (3) obtaining a print-out (diagnostic) of

22-MAR-84   SWALCAP CATALOGUING SYSTEM   FRONT END   PAGE   1
                                                    EXAMPLE PROOFSHEETS

CONTROL NO. 0-333-18691-7   LOCAL ID. sk   OWNER 4D   ON SF/CAT   ADDED   22-MAR-84   FUNCTION m   STATUS c
                                           PRV. OWNER BO ORIG. SOURCE BM   RELEASED   NOT VALIDATED
     TTT;L/R.II   REC. NO.   0

                     Dates   Country Illus   Juv GMD Form   Govt Conf Fest Inx Head Lit Biog Leng Per SF o/p Type Class
                     $ar19751974 $buk $c $d. $eW $f $g0 $h0 $i0 $j0 $k1 $lf $m $neng $o $p $qa $mn#

1 D08

2 D09   Ident Recat No o/p
                $ask $b0 $cD#

3 021 $a033316660$1bv#

4 081 $a823$b.8$c16#

5 082 $a823$b.8$c16#

6 083 $aFiction in English, 1837-1900$bTexts#

7 100   .10 $aHardy$hThomas$c1840-1928#

8 245   .10 . $aFar from the madding crowd$dThomas Hardy$fIntroduction by John Bayley, notes by Christine Winfield#

9 250   . $aNew Wessex ed.#

10 260 $aLondon$bMacmillan$c1975#

11 300 $a424p$c23cm#

12 350 $a 3.50#
                   P
13 503 $aNew Wessex ed. originally published, in pbk. 1974#

14 650 $aFiction in English#

15 690 $z11030$afiction in English$d1837-1900$z50030$atexts#

16 691 $a0000809#

17 692 $a0001686#

18 700   .11 . $aBayley$hJohn$kJohn Oliver#

19 960   R $a40 0007448 9#

20 970   R $a823.89$dR#

21 999 $hHARDY,T$tFAR FROM THE MADDING CROWDeNd74#

Diagnostic print of SWALCAP/MARC record

records for offline inspection; (4) periodical printing out of indexes, etc for consistency and validity checks. This can be a time-consuming business. 'Call-checking,' where one person 'calls out' relevant data whilst another makes visual checks for errors, is even more labour intensive. Every effort should be made, therefore, to keep mistakes to a minimum at the initial input stage.

It should also be noted that the way in which data is input may be influenced by other factors. The cataloguer will need to follow precise guidelines. A few examples should suffice to illustrate this very important point.

If a sort facility is required, for instance, it will make things complex if authors are entered as:

JOHN HUNT
ERIC SMITH
etc.

It is much easier to invert the author's name, eg:

HUNT JOHN

so that any sort on the author field will be on surname and not forename. An alternative is to place the surname and the forename in separate fields.

Similar care should be taken when handling dates. If a date is entered as Day Month Year, eg 29 1 1984, a sort by date could give a day of the month rather than a year order.

Titles can also present problems. *The ABC of archery* requires to be sorted as 'ABC ...' and not 'The ABC ...'. Similarly, *A tale of two cities* requires sorting as 'Tale ...'. If the computer is instructed to ignore 'The' and 'A', we must not be surprised if *A Level physics* sorts as 'Level physics' or if foreign articles, Le, Die, etc, are left untouched. One simple answer is to ignore articles at the beginning of titles when inputting data. The MARC format has special indicators so that the cataloguer can specify how many characters at the beginning of a title are to be disregarded when filing (see page 31).

Efficiency when searching the file must also be taken into account. An author might be entered as:

HUNT JOHN
or HUNT, JOHN

If entry is under the former, a search on the latter will produce nothing for an extra character has been added. Consistency and accuracy with regard to index terms and search terms is essential. Imagine that a periodical title has been entered as *Oppertunities* rather than *Opportunities*. In a manual index this may not matter, for a quick scan will reveal the title, despite the spelling error. A search in a machine for 'opportunities' would, however, yield a nil result.

Cataloguing rules and other standards
Some of the problems noted above will be dealt with in general cataloguing rules such as AACR2 (see page 37). These rules will, for instance, indicate that a name containing a surname, when used as an access point, is to be entered in inverted form. Selecting the form under which a name is to be entered is not quite so easy as one might imagine. How would Chiang Kai-Shek be entered, or Vincent van Gogh, or the firm W H Smith, or Tson-kha-pa Blo-bzan-grags-pa?

Cataloguing rules will also provide guidance where *choice* of name is concerned. Evan Hunter also writes as Ed McBain; which name is to be chosen as the heading for this person?

It may, of course, be unnecessary to worry about these questions. If a computer search facility is all that is required, then the names Hunter and McBain could both be entered in appropriate records so that the records will be found whichever name is looked for. A choice between the two would therefore be irrelevant and it would only become relevant if records were to be sorted by author's name or records were to be printed out under single, main author headings.

Cataloguing rules also instruct on the punctuation to be used to separate elements. A surname, for example, might be separated from a forename by a comma and a space, eg:
        WAYNE, JOHN
However, it can be superfluous and inefficient to include punctuation in every record input. It is quite easy to instruct the computer to insert any necessary punctuation when records are output. This applies equally to all the areas and elements of a bibliographic description. The International Standard Bibliographic Description (ISBD), for example, is often criticized for the rigid punctuation it prescribes to separate areas and elements. Is such provision desirable, relevant, or necessary in a machine-readable environment?

Arising from the application of rules such as AACR2 as an

aid to choice and form of access points (responsible person or body, etc), 'authority' files of names are compiled by cataloguing agencies such as the Library of Congress and the British Library which are then utilized by many other institutions.

Authority lists for the standardization of names input to machine-readable files can be of more importance than is often appreciated. When accessing a database online, it can be confusing and irritating if the name of the same person or body is found to take several different forms. Indeed, it may result in failure to retrieve relevant items. In the context of standardization for the *exchange* of bibliographic data, authority files help to ensure that names are entered in the same form by the different cooperating agencies.

Although rules for standardizing a bibliographic description and for selecting and formulating access points may be necessary, one other aspect of rules such as AACR2 is completely irrelevant in the machine-readable context. The rules will usually indicate that one of the access points should be chosen as the *main* access point or heading. This is placed over a full description to form the *main entry*. Entries under other access points are normally less detailed and these are known as *added entries*. This concept of main and added entries is redundant in the computer where *one* record is stored and the various access points merely lead to this record.

It should be noted that AACR2 does not deal with the subject approach — which is concerned with the content of an item rather than an identification or description of the physical entity. The subject may be expressed in *natural* language terms taken from the item itself and used without alteration or manipulation. This certainly could not be viewed as standardization but if the selected terms are 'translated' into 'authorized' terms as presented in a prescribed list then the indexing language is *controlled* and, if used by many agencies, could be considered as 'standard' to a degree. Classification numbers included in schemes such as the Library of Congress classification and the Dewey decimal classification comprise controlled languages, as do alphabetical terms derived from a standard list of subject headings or a thesaurus.

One further factor in relation to the standardization of a

bibliographic record remains to be mentioned. This is the requirement which may be necessary for a unique identifier for an item. It is possible to identify an item uniquely within a particular institution or agency by a running accession number. Well known examples are the Library of Congress number, eg 81-85063, and the British National Bibliography number, eg B83-23456. Although these two examples do have a certain usefulness outside the generating institution, they are not standards in the true sense of the word. Fortunately, some standards for unique identifiers do exist; examples are the International Standard Book Number (ISBN — see Glossary) and the International Standard Serial Number (ISSN) but identifiers are not available for many other forms of material. The unique identifier (if known!) offers the most efficient means of conducting a search for a particular item.

Storage of data

It is not essential for the cataloguer to be familiar with the way in which records are stored, after input, but, nevertheless, some knowledge of basic, general principles helps towards a better understanding of the overall computerized cataloguing system.

A careful examination of the sketches on pages 55 and 56 will illustrate the manner in which records are stored physically on magnetic tape and disc. Read/write heads scan the storage medium in order to enter or extract information.

Where magnetic tape is concerned, normally reading/writing can only be done when the tape is running in one direction. Records will therefore be stored *serially*, ie one after the other as added.

On the other hand, the read/write heads on the disc drives move in and out as the disc is spinning and they can therefore go to any particular spot, or address, on the disc. Thus it is possible to store the records *randomly* in whichever places are vacant.

With either tape or disc, a *sequential* physical order is possible but clearly this is more suited to the serial arrangement of the tape.

Access to magnetic tape must also be serial; all of the preceding records must be examined before a required record is reached. However, if the file is sequential, it is possible for it to be indexed so that groups of unrequired records may be skipped over. The simplest example is 'self-addressing,' where the record 'address' is also the number of its key, ie address 4 is the storage location of record 4.

With disc, access may be *direct* to a required record. This makes for much faster access than can be achieved with tape.

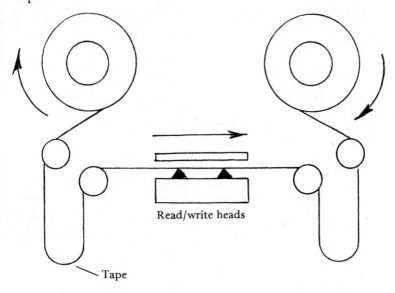

Read/write heads

Tape

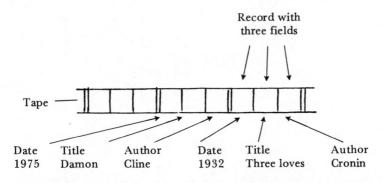

Record with
three fields

Tape

Date	Title	Author	Date	Title	Author
1975	Damon	Cline	1932	Three loves	Cronin

Sketch showing elevation of magnetic tape drive and plan of tape indicating how records are stored

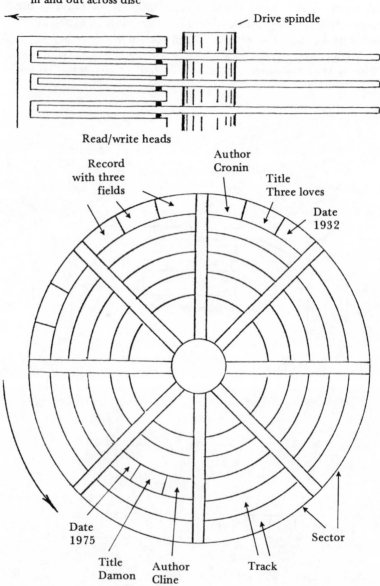

Sketch showing elevation of disc drive and plan of disc indicating how records are stored. An 'address' must specify the track and sector on the disc

Clearly storage will not be quite so simple as depicted in the above sketches. On magnetic tape, for instance, there will be a need for an inter record gap, or inter 'block of records' gap, so that the tape drive has some space, some leeway, when starting or stopping the fast moving tape.

Record 1 or first block of records		Record 2 or second block of records		Record 3 or third block of records

Inter record
or
inter block gap

Such gaps may also be present on disc and there will, of course, be a need to include certain other information such as record addresses, record lengths, and so on.

The database and file structures

The simplest form of 'database' is a single file containing just one type of record. As previously explained, it may be necessary to search through the file, record by record, in order to find the particular record(s) that contain required information. With a small file, this is perfectly feasible but larger systems will need a much faster and more flexible approach.

It is, for instance, as we have seen, possible to use a 'key' field by which the record can be found more quickly. For example, if catalogue records were ordered by author, then it would be quite easy to locate a record containing a specific author's name.

Where records need to be arranged in a key field order and they are not physically stored in this order, a system of pointers can be used to represent the required arrangement:

Start

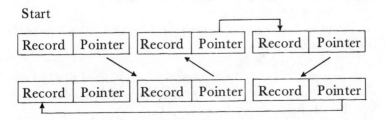

Such a structure is known as a one-way linked list and processing is always done by following the links. Because the links establish the order the data need not be continually moved as items are added or deleted.

With one-way links, there is no easy way to find the item *before* the item being examined. The chain only allows access to the record following in the order. The solution to this problem is a two-way linked list in which *two* pointers are used, one to the previous record in the list and one to the next entry. Alternatively, a circular chain can be formed. This is a linked list with the last item pointing back to the first.

As an alternative to an ordered arrangement, 'hashing' may be used. Hashing, or hash-coding, is a method of allocating records which arrive in an unpredictable order to store locations. A special algorithm, or hashing function, is used to generate a number from the characters contained in the key field, eg the author, and this number is then utilized as the block number or 'address' of the record. Hashing provides a means of fast, random access to records and removes the need for searching the file. Once the key field to be located is cited, the system can calculate the probable position and go directly to it.

Having a single 'key' will not, of course, help if a search needs to be done on some other record element. If the key field is the author field, then what if one wishes to search for a title or subject? To cater for this facility, one of the more common answers is the 'multi-indexed' system, in which a number of indices are created to point to records in the main file. One multi-indexed method often used in library type applications is the *inverted file*.

Inverted files
Whereas the normal record contains field identifiers, or attributes, together with the field contents, eg

    Author Shakespeare

an inverted list shows the *content* followed by a complete list of record identifiers, eg

    Shakespeare 1, 5, 7, etc.

A group of inverted lists comprises an inverted file and this may be completely or partially inverted depending upon whether all fields are included as lists.

MASTER FILE				
Record	Author	Title	Publisher	Date
1	MORLAND	FISHING	HAMLYN	1982
2	HANSFORD	LET'S PLAY CHESS	OCTOPUS	1980
3	EDWARDS	FISHING FOR BEGINNERS	COLLINS	1978
4	PRITCHARD	RIGHT WAY TO PLAY CHESS	ELLIOT	1950
5	STEAN	SIMPLE CHESS	FABER	1978
6	PRITCHARD	LET'S GO FISHING	OCTOPUS	1980

AUTHOR INVERTED LIST	KEYWORD FROM TITLE INVERTED LIST
EDWARDS 3 HANSFORD 2 MORLAND 1 PRITCHARD 4 6 STEAN 5	CHESS 2 4 5 FISHING 1 3 6

Partially inverted file

Complex search routines are facilitated by matching the list of identifiers for one search term against the list of identifiers for another. If searching for a book by Pritchard on chess, for example, records 4 and 6 would be matched against 2, 4 and 5 to reveal that record 4 is the only record containing both elements. Readers who have studied indexing previously may recognize that this methodology has much in common with Taube's post-coordinate system.

It is possible to link the contents of more than one field to provide some form of 'coded' search facility. Here, for example, is an inverted list under an author/title 'key' derived

from the first four letters of the author and the first three of
the title:

AUTHOR/TITLE KEY INVERTED LIST
EDWAFIS 3
HANSLET 2
MORLFIS 1
PRITLET 6
PRITRIG 4
STEASIM 5

Access vectors

In an inverted file such as that depicted on page 59, much
storage space can be wasted if provision has to be made for a
great many record numbers against each term in the inverted
list. 'Chess', for example, has three relevant record numbers
but, eventually, as the stock builds up, this may increase
considerably. It is possible to overcome the problem by using
what is referred to as an 'access vector', in which only *one*
number is stored with each term in the inverted list. This
single number reveals the start position of relevant record
numbers in a separate list.

Access vector	CHESS	1
	FISHING	4
—	ZZZ	7

Record number list	2
	4
	5
	1
	3
	6

When 'Chess' is found in the inverted list, the '1' against the term indicates that the first number in the record list is relevant and, if '1' is subtracted from the '4' against the next inverted term, this indicates that there are, in total, three relevant records. An examination of the first, second and third entries in the record list reveals that records 2, 4 and 5 are relevant.

As can be seen, the access vector needs one additional 'rogue' entry, 'ZZZ' in this case, to point one beyond the last entry in the record number list. This enables the number of relevant records for the last term in the inverted list to be calculated.

Authority files and thesauri
If vocabulary control is required, then provision for 'authority' files will have to be made, so that when an index entry is added to the system this may be compared with those already in use. Any necessary adjustment can then be made to ensure consistency and to avoid indexing the same author or subject, etc, under different forms of entry term.

    Angling
        USE FISHING

    FISHING
        Use for Angling

An alternative to a separate authority file, and possibly a more efficient means of authority control, would be to use the actual index file as the authority file, eg:

SUBJECT ACCESS INVERTED FILE
ANGLING   GO TO FISHING

CHESS
  2
  4
  5

FISHING
  1
  3
  6

If desired, both terms could be fully maintained in the access file, eg:

SUBJECT ACCESS INVERTED FILE
ANGLING
1
3
6
CHESS
2
4
5
FISHING
1
3
6

The user will automatically retrieve the same records regardless of whether 'Angling' or 'Fishing' is used as the search term.

When a subject authority list indicates more complex relationships between terms, it is referred to as a thesaurus. The following is a typical thesaurus entry; it indicates any non-preferred terms and related terms. The meanings of the abbreviations are: UF Use for; BT Broader terms; RT Related terms; NT Narrower terms.

EXPENSES
UF   Allowances
BT   Financial benefits
NT   Family allowances (provided by firm)
      Travel allowances
RT   Compensation
      Grants
      Gratuities
      Loans

Other files

In addition to index files, there may be a need for temporary workfiles used to hold records relevant to an ongoing search, a 'help' file to provide the user with assistance as required, and other related files, eg a circulation file if the catalogue is integrated with an issue system.

Field content (attribute value) tables

When a large number of records and multiple files have to be stored, the saving of space is of paramount importance. One must therefore use every possible means in order to achieve this. Some methods of data compaction are machine-based and an explanation is outside the scope of this text. A further possibility, however, is to reduce the amount of data which is to be stored. With bibliographic records, the same information, for example a particular publisher, will appear in many records and data could also be duplicated in more than one file. There is no need to waste space by storing this information over and over again. Instead, a short pointer is stored and this is linked to a look-up file which indicates field content, ie attribute value. If, for instance, the pointer for the publisher Hutchinson were 56 then the saving would be roughly 8 characters multiplied by the number of times Hutchinson was recorded in the base (less, of course, the space required by the entry in the look-up file). The look-up file will contain an ordered list of pointers indicating the corresponding publishers and possibly other terms.

MAIN FILE   ATTRIBUTE
                                            VALUE
                                            TABLE

MCCULLOUGH	AN INDECENT OBSESSION	57
BLOOM	THE CARAVAN OF CHANCE	56
WALPOLE	THE FORTRESS	55
JAGGER	THE SLEEPING SWORD	57
FORSYTH	THE ODESSA FILE	56

55 MACMILLAN
56 HUTCHINSON
57 MACDONALD

Note also the saving that might be achieved if initial articles are omitted. This is useful, for instance in a system which uses short fixed title fields, eg that of Sefton Libraries (see page 27).

More complex structures

The file organization of early data-processing systems was the simple one in which records occurred one after the other, in a known sequence, just as they might in a manual catalogue. In the subsequent 'true' database, more complicated file structures allowed for the data to be viewed in a variety of ways, depending upon the needs of the user. This more complex database therefore 'not only stores the data but shows the relationship between the various data items.'[1]

The inverted file type of structure, which has already been examined, is one form of complex database. Others are:

    Hierarchical
    Network
    Relational

The 'hierarchical' type of structure depends upon the setting up of a 'family tree' of information. The 'tree' progresses from a 'root' segment down through further segments, each segment being qualified in successive narrower and subordinate terms. The tree segments are referred to as 'nodes' and 'branches'; a branch may become a node generating further branches, thus giving rise to successive levels of hierarchy:

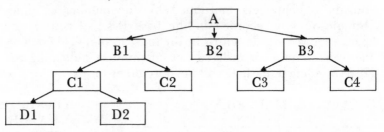

Depicted below is a bibliographic record in hierarchical structure format which should help to clarify the meaning.[2]

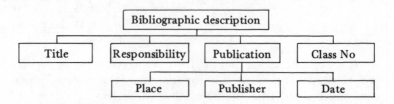

1 *Introduction to computers and information processing* / Don Cassel, Martin Jackson. – Reston, 1980
2   adapted from a similar diagram given in *Computer basics for librarians and information scientists* / Howard Fosdick. – Information Resources Press, 1981 155

For certain types of question, the hierarchical base works well but some searches may require the examination of every branch down to the lowest level. An improvement can be made if more complex links are established in which nodes with more than one 'parent' are permitted. This results in a 'network' type of structure:

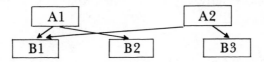

Connections can also run both ways to form an even more complex hierarchical network structure.

This is, of course, an over-simplification. The structure of a network style base can become very complex and difficult for the 'non-expert' to understand. Nevertheless, the above explanation should provide some indication of how such a structure might operate; a more detailed description is outside the scope of this work.

An even more difficult concept to understand is the 'relational' type of base, in which the links between files are 'implicit' and not 'explicit' as in the network method. The link could be, for instance, a common field in the records contained in different files:

BOOK ORDER FILE   BOOKSELLER FILE

AUTHOR	TITLE	BOOK-SELLER
Forester	Liverpool Miss	Wilson
Bogarde	Gentle occupation	Jackson

Book order file

BOOK-SELLER	REPRESEN-TATIVE	ADDRESS
Wilson	Smith	Liverpool
Jackson	Jones	Manchester

Bookseller file

Again, this is an over simplification, and, although the basic idea is simple, the relational base is a highly theoretical concept which initially required a new school of mathematical thought to describe it! It is introduced here because a number of database management systems are advertized as being 'relational' and some are described as being 'for use by', among others, 'librarians'. The true relational base provides a number of data manipulation commands (eg COMBINE, PROJECT or JOIN) that relate data in different files by the values stored in the various fields rather than by their relative positions or by pointers. The basic operations are carried out by a special relational algebra. A fully relational base offers a most flexible means of storing and controlling data and is particularly useful for the 'what if . . . ' type of enquiry.[1]

IR and DBMS

At this point it is opportune to attempt to distinguish briefly between the cataloguer's sort of database, in essence a computer-based file of bibliographic records, and the computer professional's, which is a much more general collection of data. In the former, data structure is limited, with one main file and associated indexes, code look-up files and perhaps authority files. In the latter, data structure is potentially very complex; there may be, for instance, a number of inter-related files, access between these files being facilitated by either explicit or implicit links. It may be possible to interface with other packages, for example the 1022 database management system on the DEC20 can be used with SPSS (Statistical Package for the Social Sciences), and the system may have its own programming language to allow for more sophisticated user interaction.

Loosely, the first type of base may be referred to as IR (Information Retrieval) and the second as DBMS (Data Base Management System). However, there is a 'middle ground' and some library software packages attempt to cater for this area. In addition, as Bordwell points out, there are many library operations which in fact might be sustained by DBMS.[2]

Tagg explores the differences between the two systems and concludes that in an integrated service it is unsatisfactory to offer users more than one basic method of data management and that perhaps the answer lies in a new development of

1 Database/Steve Prentice *Microcomputer printout* 3 (12) November 1982 33-48
2 dBASE II — library use of a microcomputer database management system / Stephen Bordwell *Program* 18 (2) April 1984 157-165

DBMS which incorporates the text structure requirement of free text (see page 117) databases.[1]

Finally, it should be noted that, whatever the medium or method of storage, the system should be:

1 *Fast*
   The time taken to gain access to the stored records must be short enough to be acceptable.

2 *Capacious*
   The storage capacity must be large enough to hold all the data needed during any processing run.

3 *Economic*
   The cost of storage and access must be low enough to make the system economic.

4 *Secure*
   There must be no danger of loss or damage to the stored data.

1 Bibliographic and commercial databases — contrasting approaches to data management with special reference to DBMS / Roger M. Tagg *Program* 16 (4) October 1982 191-199

Chapter Five

Manipulation of the data

Programming
The manipulation of the data within the computer is the responsibility of the person who compiles the instructions which the machine must follow. Such instructions are called *programs* and the person who writes them is referred to as a *programmer*.

The cataloguer does not need to be able to program but all cataloguers should have an awareness of what is involved in programming.

We have seen how the computer operates in binary mode and, at the lowest level, instructions could be given in this 'machine language'. A binary coded instruction would therefore appear as a pattern of 1s and 0s, eg:

0001 0000

It is quite difficult to learn how to write such machine coded instructions, although, at one time, computer operators had to learn this language. Today, it is possible to write instructions in a 'high level' language which uses familiar English words combined with punctuation marks, mathematical expressions, or symbols. The high level language has to be 'translated' into pure binary by the machine itself before the instructions can be understood and implemented.

Here is an example of a simple instruction written in the high level language PASCAL:

WRITE ('ENTER AUTHOR')

This would cause the words ENTER AUTHOR to appear

on the vdu screen at an appropriate point in a program.

The same instruction, written in the high level language COBOL, would be:

```
DISPLAY "ENTER AUTHOR"
```

There are some hundreds of different high level languages. Either of the two cited above could be used for database management applications. Currently, however, the best known language is BASIC (Beginners' All-purpose Symbolic Instruction Code). This is by far the most common 'resident' microcomputer language and it is also available on mainframes. It is a fairly easy language to understand and is often taught, to an elementary level, in library schools. It will therefore be used here to help illustrate how programming may be applied to cataloguing applications. It should be appreciated, however, that BASIC is not perhaps the best choice of language for library operations.

BASIC – Input and output

In BASIC, each instruction or *statement* is allocated a line number and the computer carries out instructions in line number order. A program will usually begin with a REMark statement which is merely a comment and which is not acted upon by the computer, eg:

```
10  REM *** PROGRAM TO ENTER AND PRINT OUT A
         CATALOGUE ENTRY ***
```

This particular REMark tells us what the program is intended to do. In addition to REM, this first, brief illustrative program, which is shown in full below, uses three other statements:

INPUT   which permits the entry of data into the computer's store

PRINT   which enables the display of instructions and data on the vdu screen

END   which indicates the completion of a program

```
10  REM *** PROGRAM TO ENTER AND PRINT OUT A
         CATALOGUE ENTRY ***
20  PRINT "ENTER AUTHOR (SURNAME ONLY)"
30  INPUT AUTHOR$
```

```
 40  PRINT "ENTER AUTHOR (FORENAME—S)"
 50  INPUT FORENAME$
 60  PRINT "ENTER TITLE"
 70  INPUT TITLE$
 80  PRINT "ENTER PUBLISHER"
 90  INPUT PUBLISHER$
100  PRINT "ENTER DATE"
110  INPUT DATE
120  PRINT "ENTER CLASS NO"
130  INPUT CLASS$
140  PRINT
150  PRINT
160  PRINT
170  PRINT AUTHOR$;", ";FORENAME$;"."
180  PRINT "   ";TITLE$;"."
190  PRINT "   ";PUBLISHER$;", ";DATE;"."
200  PRINT
210  PRINT "                    ";CLASS$
220  END
```

The input of the data to the computer's store is accomplished by lines 20 to 130. The computer will relate each string of characters input at a particular point to the name allocated by the programmer, eg AUTHOR$ will relate to the author's name. The $ indicates that the string of characters will be a textual string. A number, eg DATE, does not require the dollar sign.

The output of the catalogue entry is controlled by lines 170 to 210. The machine will output each string of characters in the position indicated by the name allocated to it and will interpose, between each element, the punctuation or spaces which appear in inverted commas. Lines 140 to 160 print blank lines (before the output of the entry) as does line 200 (within the entry itself).

To operate the program the command:

    RUN

would be used and on the vdu screen would then appear:

    ENTER AUTHOR (SURNAME ONLY)

Suppose that

    MILLETT

were input, the computer would then respond with:

ENTER AUTHOR (FORENAME–S)

and

FRED B

could then be input. The program would continue to run in this manner until the complete record had been entered. A print out of the full record would then appear, printed in accordance with the program instructions and with the appropriate punctuation and spacing inserted:

MILLETT, FRED B.
   READING FICTION.
   HARPER, 1950.
        823

The above program, although realistic in the sense that it would work, is obviously merely illustrative of the way in which an entry might be input and output. In practice, many entries would be involved.

Consider the following program extract:

```
10  DIM AUTHOR$(500), TITLE$(500)
20  FOR COUNT = 1 TO 500
30  PRINT "ENTER AUTHOR"
40  INPUT AUTHOR$(COUNT)
50  PRINT "ENTER TITLE"
60  INPUT TITLE$(COUNT)
70  NEXT COUNT
```

This depicts what is known in programming terminology as a 'loop', which is a repeating mechanism. The DIMension statement in line 10 informs the computer that space should be reserved for a list of five hundred authors and titles. The variable COUNT progressively increases from 1 through to 500. After each author and title has been input, the program switches from line 70 back to line 20 to permit the next input. The complete cycle allows for the entry of up to five hundred authors and titles identified within the computer as AUTHOR$(1) and TITLE$(1), AUTHOR$(2) and TITLE$(2), AUTHOR$(3) and TITLE$(3), etc.

An escape route from the loop would be provided using a

'rogue' string, ie one that would not be encountered in practice, to cater for the fact that all of the data might not be entered at the one time, eg:

```
45 IF AUTHOR$(COUNT) = "EOF" THEN GOTO 80
```

If the user enters EOF (ie End of File) at any point, when prompted for an author, the program would switch to line 80 and begin the next stage of the operation.

Note that the reason why line numbers increase in increments of ten (or even one hundred) is so that additional statements can be interposed as the program is developed.

A similar loop to that shown above would be used to output the data when, and if required.

Not only does data have to be input and output but, between these two operations, it has to be manipulated according to requirement. Two of the 'manipulations' most relevant to cataloguing are sorting and searching. How are these achieved?

BASIC – Sorting

As we have seen, every character is allocated a value within the machine. Numerals usually have less value than letters; punctuation marks have various values; a space has the least value of all. If, for example, A = 65, B = 66 and C = 67 then:

A is less than B or C

B is less than C

Strings of characters are 'read', character by character, from left to right, so that:

AB is less than BA

and

ABC is less than ACB

It follows that, for instance:

BLAKE is less than LAMB

LAMB is less than WALKER

WALKER is less than WALLER

This is the secret of how the computer can sort alphabetically. Statements such as:

IF "BLAKE" < "LAMB" THEN . . .

or

IF AUTHOR$(1) < AUTHOR$(2) THEN . . .

where the relational operator < (see Glossary) means 'is less than', are perfectly valid in BASIC.

A computer can therefore be instructed to examine a list of authors, titles, etc, compare adjacent names, and switch them if they are not in the correct order. A series of passes through the list may need to be made, eg:

Original order	First pass	Second pass	Third pass
JAWS	JAWS	JAWS	EXODUS
MACBETH	KIDNAPPED	EXODUS	JAWS
KIDNAPPED	EXODUS	KES	KES
EXODUS	KES	KIDNAPPED	KIDNAPPED
KES	MACBETH	MACBETH	MACBETH

This is the common 'bubble' sort, in which the highest or the lowest 'values' rise to the top like bubbles in a liquid. This is not the fastest or the best algorithm for sorting but the methodology is reasonably easy to understand.

In the first pass JAWS is compared with MACBETH and no exchange is made as they are in the correct alphabetical order. MACBETH is then compared with KIDNAPPED and an exchange is necessary and is therefore made. MACBETH is now in the position that KIDNAPPED previously occupied and it is therefore compared with EXODUS and exchanged, and then KES and exchanged. Thus at the end of the pass, MACBETH becomes the last item in the list. At the end of the second pass, the next to last item must be the next to last in alphabetical order, in this case KIDNAPPED. This process continues until the complete list is in the required alphabetical order.

Here is a short bubble sort BASIC program, which permits the input of up to 500 character strings. These are then sorted and output in alphabetical order:

```
10   REM *** BUBBLE SORT ***
20   DIM STRING$(500)
30   FOR C = 1 TO 500
40   PRINT "ENTER STRING ";C
50   INPUT STRING$(C)
60   IF STRING$(C) = "ZZZ" THEN LET N = C−1 : GOTO 80
70   NEXT C
80   REM *** SORT ROUTINE ***
90   FOR J = 1 TO N−1
100  FOR K = 1 TO N−1
```

```
110  IF STRING$(K) < STRING$(K+1) THEN GOTO 150
120  LET X$ = STRING$(K)
130  LET STRING$(K) = STRING$(K+1)
140  LET STRING$(K+1) = X$
150  NEXT K
160  NEXT J
170  PRINT
180  PRINT "ALPHABETICAL LISTING"
190  PRINT
200  FOR L = 1 TO N
210  PRINT STRING$(L)
220  NEXT L
230  END
```

The input and output routines are similar to those previously described, except that a LET statement in line 60 relates the number of strings entered (C−1) to the variable N. The hub of the program is contained in 80 to 160. The 'inner' loop 100−150 performs one 'pass' through the list, interchanging strings if they are not in alphabetical order. The actual exchange takes place in lines 120−140 where use is made of a temporary 'store' X$. The outer loop 90−160 controls the number of passes through the list. The number of 'comparisons' in each pass must obviously equal one less than the number of strings to be sorted, ie N−1. The number of passes that might be necessary will vary according to the original order but the maximum number will be the number required when the original order is the complete reverse of the final order. This will also equal N−1.

It is not unusual to find one loop 'nested' within another as in the above program. The device will be used later for the input of data, the outer loop controlling the list of records and the inner the fields within each record.

BASIC − Searching
Searching, like sorting, can be done within the computer in a variety of ways. The simplest method is to look through a list, item by item, to see if there is a 'match' with the search term. This can again be achieved by a loop, eg

```
100  PRINT "ENTER REQUIRED AUTHOR"
110  INPUT REQ$
```

```
120  FOR C = 1 TO 500
130  IF AUTHOR$(C) = REQ$ THEN PRINT AUTHOR$(C),
     TITLE$(C)
140  NEXT C
```

Code	Character	Code	Character
32		63	?
33	!	64	@
34	"	65	A
35	#	66	B
36	$	67	C
37	%	68	D
38	&	69	E
39	'	70	F
40	(	71	G
41	)	72	H
42	*	73	I
43	+	74	J
44	,	75	K
45	—	76	L
46	.	77	M
47	/	78	N
48	0	79	O
49	1	80	P
50	2	81	Q
51	3	82	R
52	4	83	S
53	5	84	T
54	6	85	U
55	7	86	V
56	8	87	W
57	9	88	X
58	:	89	Y
59	;	90	Z
60	<	91	[
61	=	92	\
62	>	93	]

Part of the ASCII (American Standard Code for Information Interchange) character set showing rank order of symbols, digits, letters, etc. Omitted characters include lower case letters (codes 97 to 122)

The above program extract would work through a list of authors and titles to see if any particular author – AUTHOR$(C) – matched the author required – REQ$. If a match is found, line 130 outputs the relevant author and title.

A serial search like that shown above is slow and cumbersome. A much faster search can be achieved if the data is ordered first. For example, if we are looking for DENT in an ordered list of five hundred authors, DENT could first be compared with the author in the middle of the list (position 250). If the author in this position were MORRISON then it would be known immediately that DENT *must* precede this author and the last 250 entries in the list have therefore been eliminated from the search at a stroke! The first 250 entries can then be examined by comparing DENT with the author in position 125. If this author were HINTON then authors 125 through to 250 have been eliminated. Proceeding in this way, it can very quickly be ascertained whether DENT is in the list or not. This is known as binary chop searching.

If a binary search routine is combined with an inverted file (see page 58), in which ordered indexes to a main file are maintained, then we are moving towards a very efficient search routine.

A complete cataloguing system
A complete cataloguing system would need to contain, at the least, the following elements:

1 Creation of the file
2 Display of the file
3 Addition to the file
4 Amendment of the file
5 Deletion from the file
6 Search of the file

A further module might be necessary, ie

7 Sorting and printing out the file

but, if an online user search facility was all that was required, then sorting for output would be superfluous, although sorting would still be used as necessary within the program, eg to cater for faster searching.

Sub-modules would also form an integral part of the

system. For example, a choice could be given between displaying a single record or scrolling a complete section of the file.

The creation of the file could be accomplished in a similar manner to that described on page 71, ie a loop could be used to input a list and each record element would be identified by a number, eg AUTHOR\$(1), TITLE\$(1), AUTHOR\$(2), TITLE\$(2), etc. The number within the parentheses is known as a 'subscript'. The subscripts introduced so far have been single numbers and a single number implies a one-dimensional list or array. However, two-dimensional lists can be useful for cataloguing applications. For example, in BASIC, a two-dimensional array R\$(N,F) could be set up, where R is a mnemonic name for 'Record' and where N is the record number and F is the field number within the record. It is convenient to view this as a matrix of rows (N) and columns (F), eg:

		F			
	0	1	2	3	4
0	AUTHOR	TITLE	PUBLISHER	DATE	CLASS
1	MALINS	UNDERSTANDING PAINTINGS	PHAIDON	1980	751
2	SODERBERG	POPULAR PET KEEPING	ELLIOT	1950	636
3	CARR	LAWNS	EBURY	1981	635
4	HOUSBY	BOAT FISHING	PAN	1971	799
5	DAWSON	CARD GAMES	WILLS	1933	793

(N labels the rows 1–5 on the left)

The field names are 'concealed' in the zero subscript row and the record numbers therefore begin, correctly, at one.

The use of such an array makes it easy to refer to a particular record, or the name and content of a specific field in a particular record, thus R\$(0,1) = TITLE and R\$(2,1) is the title of the second record, ie *Popular pet keeping.*

Here is a program segment for the input of such a list, which would contain up to 1,000 records:

```
1000  REM *** CREATING THE FILE ***
1010  PRINT "WHAT IS FILE NAME?"
1020  INPUT FILE$
1030  REM ** MAXIMUM SIZE OF FILE **
1040  DIM R$(1000,5)
1050  REM ** ALLOCATION OF FIELD NAMES **
```

```
1060  LET R$(0,0) = "AUTHOR" : R$(0,1) = "TITLE" :
         R$(0,2) = "PUBLISHER" : R$(0,3) = "DATE" :
         R$(0,4) = "CLASS"
1070  REM ** ENTERING THE DATA **
1080  FOR N = 1 TO 1000
1090  PRINT "ENTER DATA. WHEN FINISHED ENTER EOF
         AS AUTHOR"
1100  PRINT
1110  PRINT "ENTER RECORD ";N
1120  FOR F = 0 TO 4
1130  PRINT "ENTER ";R$(0,F)
1140  INPUT R$(N,F)
1150  IF R$(N,F) = "EOF" THEN GOTO 1180
1160  NEXT F
1170  NEXT N
1180  REM *** END OF CREATION CYCLE ***
```

To display a record, after input, a simple routine such as the following could be used:

```
2000  *** DISPLAYING A RECORD ***
2010  PRINT "WHAT IS NUMBER OF RECORD REQUIRED?"
2020  INPUT X
2030  PRINT
2040  PRINT "REC NO ";X
2050  FOR F = 0 TO 4
2060  PRINT R$(O,F), R$(X,F)
2070  NEXT F
```

If, for instance, record number 4 were asked for, the resultant output would be:

```
REC NO 4
AUTHOR      HOUSBY
TITLE       BOAT FISHING
PUBLISHER   PAN
DATE        1971
CLASS       799
```

Obviously, records would not be entered all at once and additions to the file would have to be catered for. This would necessitate an amendment to the file creation routine.

Line 1080 could more usefully read:

```
1080  FOR N = C TO 1000
```

"C" would be initially set at 1, ie

```
1075  LET C = 1
```

but would progressively increase each time the file creation routine was used. This is achieved by making C equal to N after EOF has been entered, ie:

```
1150  IF R$(N,F) = "EOF" THEN LET C = N : GOTO 1180
```

Thus, if, subsequently, the cataloguer indicated that he/she wished to add to the file, a GOTO 1080 statement is all that would be required and the creation loop would begin at the next record number.

The amendment of a record in the file could be achieved as follows:

```
4000  *** AMENDING A RECORD ***
4010  PRINT "WHAT IS NUMBER OF RECORD TO BE
      AMENDED?"
4020  INPUT Y
4030  PRINT
4040  FOR F = 0 TO 4
4050  PRINT R$(O,F), R$(Y,F)
4060  PRINT
4070  PRINT "ANY AMENDMENT? YES/NO"
4080  INPUT D$
4090  IF D$ = "NO" THEN GOTO 4150
4100  PRINT
4120  PRINT "ENTER AMENDED ";R$(O,F)
4130  INPUT M$
4140  LET R$(Y,F) = M$
4150  NEXT F
```

The above routine would display each field of the record to be altered in turn and ask whether any amendment was necessary. If the answer were "No' the next field would be displayed and the same question asked. This sequence would

continue until the answer was 'Yes', in which case lines 4120
to 4140 would permit the field content to be changed.

If a record was to be deleted from the file, this could be
done by reducing the number of all the subsequent records in
the file by one:

```
5000 *** DELETING A RECORD ***
5010 PRINT "WHAT IS NUMBER OF RECORD TO BE
     DELETED?"
5020 INPUT Z
5030 FOR N = Z TO C-1
5040 FOR F = 0 TO 4
5050 LET R$(N,F) = R$(N+1,F)
5060 NEXT F
5070 NEXT N
```

The record following the record to be deleted is moved
into its place and the deleted record therefore 'disappears'.

A serial search of the file could be carried out as explained
on page 74 but with the variable names changed to conform
to those now used, ie

```
6000 *** SEARCHING THE FILE ***
6010 PRINT "ENTER REQUIRED AUTHOR"
6020 INPUT A$
6030 FOR N = 1 TO C-1
6040 IF R$(N,O) <> A$ THEN GOTO 6100
6050 PRINT
6060 PRINT "REC NO ";N
6070 FOR F = 0 TO 4
6080 PRINT R$(O,F),R$(N,F)
6090 NEXT F
6100 NEXT N
```

In the above routine the outer loop (lines 6030 to 6100)
searches through the list looking at each author. If an author
is not equal to the search term then no action is taken (note
that <> means not equal to, ie less than or greater than) but
if a match is found then lines 6060 to 6090 print out the
number and details of the relevant record.

Searching need not, of course, be restricted to the
author. The user could be given a choice of fields to search.

Line 6040 would have to be changed to:

```
6040  IF R$(N,F) ...
```

and F could be set to 0, 1, 2, etc, according to which field was required.

If faster and more sophisticated searching was required, the file creation module would need to be expanded to allow for the input of index terms into one or more inverted lists (see page 58) as each record is entered. The inverted lists could be ordered using an 'insertion' sort, which places each term into its correct place as entered. Access vectors (see page 60) could also be used.

If sorting of the file was a requisite, it is unlikely that the bubble sort shown on page 73 would be used. As previously stated, there are much faster methods which can be employed. One point to remember is that it is not sufficient to sort just one field, *all* of the elements of the records must be 'sorted' at the same time. In other words, record components must stay together.

Note that if a file has been sorted on some field other than the first, it is quite easy to rearrange the output so that the sorted element is displayed at the beginning. For example, if records had been sorted by title:

```
FOR T = 1 TO C−1
PRINT R$(0,1), R$(T,1)
PRINT R$(0,0), R$(T,0)
PRINT R$(0,2), R$(T,2)
PRINT R$(0,3), R$(T,3)
PRINT R$(0,4), R$(T,4)
NEXT T
```

One essential feature of any file handling program is a facility to save the files on tape or disc and load them back into the computer's immediate access memory, in whole or in part, as and when necessary. A full explanation of how to do this is, however, outside the scope of this work. Nor does space permit of a detailed explanation of the programming for some of the other possibilities mentioned above, eg binary searching or insertion sorting of an inverted list. In addition, many facilities which are available in BASIC, some of which are either essential or extremely useful in cataloguing applications, have not been mentioned at all. Examples are *subroutines*, which are sections of a program which can be called up again and again as required, and character string functions. The latter provide a means of breaking down, building up, or searching through character strings. Further, the program extracts that have been included here have been written for ease of understanding rather than for sophistication of programming technique. Nevertheless, enough information has been supplied, hopefully, to help achieve the major objective of making cataloguers aware of what is involved in the programmer's task.

Chapter Six

Output of the data

When an institution or agency has stored its cataloguing data in a computer, this data can be output, after manipulation, in one of two ways:

1 As an entity.
2 Record by record (or section by section) as required.

Output as an entity would only occur when the resultant complete catalogue was to be searched *offline*.

Computer produced physical forms for offline access

There are, in essence, three major computer produced physical forms which are of relevance to offline access:

1 Printed book
   Entries are printed as text in a conventional book-type format available in multiple copies.
2 Card
   Each entry is recorded on one or more cards of standard size (12.5 × 7.5 cm) and the cards are then filed in drawers housed in catalogue cabinets.
3 Microform
   Entries are greatly reduced and 'printed' upon film. A suitable 'reader' which magnifies the film and projects it on to a screen is required (the larger and the busier the library, the greater the number of copies of the catalogue and hence the greater the number of readers that will be necessary).
   Microfilm may be on a single reel but, more usually, it is housed in a cassette containing two reels so that

the film can be wound backwards and forwards within its container. Microfilm may come in:

comic mode, ie

P1	P2	P3	P4	P5	P6

or *cine mode*, ie

P1
P2
P3
P4
P5
P6

Microfilm readers will, therefore, often allow rotation of the image through 90 degrees.

Microfiche, nowadays much more common than microfilm for catalogue use, is a transparent 'card' type format. A reduction of 42X gives 200 frames per card.

Microfiche can also be presented in comic or cine mode and is very often in double column format:

comic mode

P 1 Col 1	Col 2	P 2 Col 1	Col 2	P 3 Col 1	Col 2

cine mode

P 1 Col 1	Col 2
P 2 Col 1	Col 2
P 3 Col 1	Col 2

Microfiche has the advantage of direct access to a particular frame whereas microfilm requires a 'serial' search through the film to find a relevant entry.

The first two of the above forms may be produced by using the computer print-out itself as a master and then reproducing (and perhaps reducing) this master by xerography or some other means. Photocomposition can also be used, the print master, in this case, being a photographic negative.

```
BISHOP, Peter
    Computer programming in BASIC / Peter
Bishop. - Walton-on-Thames : Nelson, 1978.
    140 p. ; 24 cm.
    ISBN 0-17-431270-9.
```

QA76.73B3

```
FORSYTH, Richard
    The BASIC idea : an introduction to
computer programming / Richard Forsyth. -
London : Chapman and Hall, 1978.
    vi,154 p. ; 22 cm.
    With answers to selected exercises.
    ISBN 0-470-99397-9.
```

QA76.73B3

```
MEEK, Brian
    Using computers / Brian Meek, Simon
Fairthorne. - Chichester : Ellis Horwood,
1977.
    208 p. : ill. ; 24 cm.
    Bibliography: p.199-202.
    ISBN 0-85312-045-5.
```

QA76

```
SANDERSON, Peter C.
    Introduction to microcomputer
programming / Peter C. Sanderson. -
London : Newnes, 1980.
    138 p. ; 22 cm.
    Includes BASIC, assembly and machine
code and provides suggested solutions
to exercises.
    ISBN 0-408-00415-0.
```

QA76.6

```
TROMBETTA, Michael
    BASIC for students : with applications /
Michael Trombetta. - Reading, Mass. :
Addison-Wesley, 1981.
    xi, 291 p. ; 24 cm.
    ISBN 0-201-07611-X.
```

QA76.73B3

Catalogue entries output on lineprinter and then reduced using xerography. Those entries shown here are in AACR2 format (see page 30)

Where (3) is concerned, computer output on magnetic tape can be automatically processed into a microform (COM — Computer Output Microform). Such processing is normally done by commercial agencies, although machines can be purchased for in-house use.

The three offline formats noted above must be regarded as *interim* formats; eventually all catalogues will be searched online. There is, indeed, something paradoxical about the power of a computer being used to produce catalogue cards. Thus a very advanced process is followed by tedious manual filing in the monstrous space eaters which the card catalogues of large libraries have become.

At least, with the printed book and the microform (which is, after all, merely a 'printed' format very much reduced in size) no manual filing of entries is necessary.

The small size of the microform also offers another advantage, the possibility of including additional access points such as keywords from the title (see also page 91).

One of the greatest disadvantages of all of these offline forms is the fact that they are always out of date, although the use of the computer does mean that catalogue cards can be produced quickly for manual filing and that revised printed book and microform catalogues can be updated at regular intervals. This applies particularly to the microform as this is much less expensive. Some libraries issue new versions of their complete microform catalogue as often as once a month.

Presentation

The way in which a catalogue is *presented* to the user, in terms of guiding, layout and typography, is most important.

The user must be able to find the information that is required as quickly and as conveniently as possible. It must be easy to:

1 Find the relevant place in the catalogue.
2 Find the relevant specific entry/entries.
3 Find any relevant element within an entry.

(1) demands explicit instructions relating to the use of the catalogue and adequate external and internal guiding.

(2) demands a clear layout with entries separated from one another and with lead terms, or elements under which the entries are filed, given prominence.

(3) demands the use of spacing, punctuation, paragraphing, etc, as necessary.

The printed book is relatively easy to guide. It can be

externally 'labelled' and contain internal detail of content and instructions for use. The computer can be programmed to produce page and column headings, indexes, etc. The user will be reasonably familiar with the book format and will therefore find it comparatively simple to handle.

The card catalogue requires prominent, clear and accurate external guides, both general and specific (eg to individual drawers), and effective internal guiding such as guide cards (ie with protruding tabs). Different coloured cards for different types of entry, sequences or materials, may be helpful. Such guiding cannot, however, be automatically produced and placed in position by the computer; it necessitates manual insertion with all of the possible errors and pitfalls that this entails.

The microform catalogue must incorporate in its general instructions guidance on how to insert the film or fiche into the reader for examination. It is obviously important to have readers which are easy to use. Access to film is strictly sequential whereas, with fiche, the user can move directly from frame to frame as already noted. The latter can be somewhat confusing at first, especially if, as with some fiche catalogues, reading is from right to left rather than from left to right. The fiche may have an index to frames in one corner in the hope that this will facilitate access.

The microfilm merely requires each cassette or reel to be adequately labelled and further guiding can be internal. Fiche is more problematic because it involves the selection of the appropriate fiche from a binder or some other holder and then the reinsertion of the fiche into its correct position after use. Selection should be facilitated by clear labelling of each fiche. It is the author's opinion that this is not always as adequate as it might perhaps be. A fiche title includes varied information such as the name of the library, type of catalogue, date, etc. However, the most important item is the position of the particular fiche in the overall sequence, eg "From DELTA to DONNE", and this should be as large and as clear as possible. Reinsertion of the fiche into its correct place clearly demands co-operative users and every effort should be made to make this chore as 'painless' as possible. One helpful aid is the 'anti-misfiling' colour strip which is illustrated on page 89.

One very important point that should be stressed is that

the frames of a microform should not be packed and crammed with information. Enough space should be left so that the result is acceptable to the human eye. It is possible, for example, using Computer Output Microform, to have line lengths of well over one hundred characters but this is far too many and line length should be restricted to about 60 characters. The number of lines per page should also be restricted to between 60 and 70.[1] It should be remembered that the catalogue is to be projected onto a screen and therefore, in addition to the above factors, the largest size of character available should be chosen.

Using a microfiche catalogue

1 *Visual presentation of information in COM library catalogues* / L. Reynolds. — British Library, 1979. — (British Library research and development report ; no.5472). — 2 v. Vol. 1 7

CHESHIRE LIBRARIES	ADULT NON-FICTION CATALOGUE	AUTHOR	FROM AAAAA TO ALMOND	02/01/83	0001
CHESHIRE LIBRARIES	ADULT NON-FICTION CATALOGUE	AUTHOR	FROM ALMOND TO ASHE	02/01/83	0002
CHESHIRE LIBRARIES	ADULT NON-FICTION CATALOGUE	AUTHOR	FROM ASHE TO BAKER	02/01/83	0003
CHESHIRE LIBRARIES	ADULT NON-FICTION CATALOGUE	AUTHOR	FROM BAKER TO BASS	02/01/83	0004
CHESHIRE LIBRARIES	ADULT NON-FICTION CATALOGUE	AUTHOR	FROM BASS TO BELL	02/01/83	0005
CHESHIRE LIBRARIES	ADULT NON-FICTION CATALOGUE	AUTHOR	FROM BELL TO BIRKET	02/01/83	0006
CHESHIRE LIBRARIES	ADULT NON-FICTION CATALOGUE	AUTHOR	FROM BIRKET TO BORODI	02/01/83	0007
CHESHIRE LIBRARIES	ADULT NON-FICTION CATALOGUE	AUTHOR	FROM BORODI TO BRIDGE	02/01/83	0008
CHESHIRE LIBRARIES	ADULT NON-FICTION CATALOGUE	AUTHOR	FROM BRIDGE TO BROWN	02/01/83	0009
CHESHIRE LIBRARIES	ADULT NON-FICTION CATALOGUE	AUTHOR	FROM BROWN TO BUTLER	02/01/83	0010
CHESHIRE LIBRARIES	ADULT NON-FICTION CATALOGUE	AUTHOR	FROM BUTLER TO CARTER	02/01/83	0011
CHESHIRE LIBRARIES	ADULT NON-FICTION CATALOGUE	AUTHOR	FROM CARTER TO CHERWE	02/01/83	0012
CHESHIRE LIBRARIES	ADULT NON-FICTION CATALOGUE	AUTHOR	FROM CHERWE TO CLEMEN	02/01/83	0013
CHESHIRE LIBRARIES	ADULT NON-FICTION CATALOGUE	AUTHOR	FROM CLEMEN TO CONNOL	02/01/83	0014
CHESHIRE LIBRARIES	ADULT NON-FICTION CATALOGUE	AUTHOR	FROM CONNOL TO COX AN	02/01/83	0015
CHESHIRE LIBRARIES	ADULT NON-FICTION CATALOGUE	AUTHOR	FROM COX-IF TO DANIEL	02/01/83	0016

Part of Cheshire Libraries (UK) microfiche catalogue showing 'anti-misfiling' colour strip

ADULT   NON-FICTION   AUTHOR CATALOGUE   (SUPL)   PAGE 00085 24/03/84

BAY - BEA

BAYLISS, ROBERT   694   THE BBC MICRO TOOLBOX: AIDS TO MORE EFFICIENT
CARPENTRY AND JOINERY. VOL.1. HUTCHINSON, 1961. 694.   PROGRAMMING, BY IAN TRACKMAN. BBC SOFT, 1983. BOOKLET   SCU.001642
~B   AND MICROCOMPUTER CASSETTE FOR BBC MODEL B.
B 61009954   ==   £ 0.00   3R,4M,4S,6C   GT   £ 18.26
                           0 563 21058 3

BAYLISS, R   694.   BBC MODEL A AND B
CARPENTRY & JOINERY O2. REV. & METRICATED ED. HUTCHINSON.   EARLY LEARNING: 5 MATHS AND SPELLING PROGRAMS
1970 REPRINT. ILLUS.   FOR CHILDREN. BBC SOFT, 1982. BOOKLET AND MICROCOMPUTER
1A,2B,2G,2J,7M,7Z   CASSETTE FOR BBC MODEL A AND B.
0 09097 931 1   ==   £ 1.95   SEE EARLY LEARNING: 5 MATHS AND SPELLING PROGRAMS
                                      FOR CHILDREN. BBC SOFT, 1982 BOOKLET AND MICROCOMPUTER
BAYLOR, H.W.   CASSETTE FOR BBC MODEL A AND B.
ILL.
SINCERE'S HISTORY OF THE SEWING MACHINE. SINCER P., 1970.
SEE EWERS, WILLIAM   BBC MODEL B
                                 THE BBC MICRO TOOLBOX: AIDS TO MORE EFFICIENT
BAYNES, KEN   629.0460221   PROGRAMMING, BY IAN TRACKMAN. BBC SOFT, 1983. BOOKLET
THE ART OF THE ENGINEER. KEN BAYNES AND FRANCIS PUGH.   AND MICROCOMPUTER CASSETTE FOR BBC MODEL B.
LUTTERWORTH, 1981. 240P. ILLISOME COL.).   SEE THE BBC MICRO TOOLBOX: AIDS TO MORE EFFICIENT
2E.4D   PROGRAMMING, BY IAN TRACKMAN. BBC SOFT, 1983. BOOKLET
0 7188 2506 3   ==   £ 28.00   AND MICROCOMPUTER CASSETTE FOR BBC MODEL B.

BAYNES, KEN   749.22   BBC MODEL B
GORDON RUSSELL. DESIGN COUNCIL, 1980. ILL.~   WHITE KNIGHT MK.II: THE BBC CHESS MASTER
2x   BY MARTIN BRYANT. BBC SOFT, 1983. BOOKLET AND MICROCOMPUTE
0 85072 119 9   £ 5.00   CASSETTE FOR BBC MODEL B.
                                 SEE WHITE KNIGHT MK.II: THE BBC CHESS MASTER
BAYNES, J   942.071   BY MARTIN BRYANT. BBC SOFT, 1983. BOOKLET AND MICROCOMPUTE
THE JACOBITE RISING OF 1715. CASSELL, 1970. ILLUS. BIBLIOG.   CASSETTE FOR BBC MODEL B.
1R,2B,4B,4D2,4M,4Z
0 304 93565 4   BH   £ 2.25   BBC WRITING AND SPELLING HANDBOOK. EDITED BY   808.042
                                 CATHERINE MOORHOUSE. BBC, 1979. ILL.
BAYNES, HELTON GODWIN   157.282   1R,2B2,2G,2H,2M,2T,3E2,3J,3R,4D5,4F,4G,4L,4M,4S3,4W4,6C2,6H,
MYTHOLOGY OF THE SOUL. A RESEARCH INTO THE UNCONSCIOUS FROM   6J2,7M,7W2,7Z2
SCHIZOPHRENIC DREAMS AND DRAWINGS. (NEW ED.). RIDER, 1969.   0 563 16262 9   GT   £ 1.99
1R
0 09 098740 3   ==   £ 0.00   BEACH BOYS   AKA.33454
                                 BEST OF THE BEACH BOYS.
BAYNES, K   385.0207   2E.2T
THE RAILWAY CARTOON BOOK. DAVID & C. 1976. IL..   EMI ST 20856.
4M2,7S,7T,7W   C 0144273 2   £ 2.09
0 7153 7354 4   TT   £ 2.95
                                 BEACH BOYS   AKA.27062
THE BBC GUIDE TO PARLIAMENT 1983. BBC, 1983.   328.41   ENDLESS SUMMER: 20 CLASSIC TRACKS.
                                 EMI MFP 50528.
                                 4W   £ 2.06
4E,6J2,7Z   C 01283596
0 563 20245 9   GT   £ 7.25   BEACH BOYS   AKA.21998
                                 GIRLS ON THE BEACH.
                                 CAPITOL CAPS 1037.
                                 4D,4W,6J
                                 C 0106626 6   £ 3.00

J 6

LIVERPOOL POLYTECHNIC : ALPHABETIC CATALOGUE MAY 1984

D- 4

CAM MECHANISMS
CAMS AND CAM MECHANISMS: PROC. OF MECHANISMS 74 CONFERENCE /
organ. by Institution Of Mechanical Engineers ; ed. by Rees
Jones,J. - Mech. Eng. Pub., 1978 £34.09 0-85298-361-1
SHELVED AT 621.838 CON EXCEPT WHERE INDICATED:
yrom St.: 2 copies

CAM MECHANISMS
DESIGN OF CAM MECHANISMS AND LINKAGES / by Molian,S. -
Constable, 1968 x-85-047735-1
SHELVED AT 621.838 MOL EXCEPT WHERE INDICATED:
Byrom St.: 2 copies

CAM MECHANISMS
KINEMATICS AND GEOMETRY OF PLANAR AND SPATIAL CAM MECHANISMS /
by Chakraoorty,J. and Dhande,S.G. - Wiley, 1977 £4.50 0-
85226-116-0
SHELVED AT 621.838 CHA EXCEPT WHERE INDICATED:
Byrom St.: 2 copies

CAMACHO, G.
LATIN AMERICA: A SHORT HISTORY / by Camacho,G. - Allen Lane,
1973 x-85-092482-x
SHELVED AT 980 CAM EXCEPT WHERE INDICATED:
Walton Ho. Reserve: 1 copy

CAMACHO, M.
CHARLAS EN LA PRISION: EL MOVIMIENTO OBRERO SINDICAL / by
Camacho,M. - Lib. Du Globe, 1974 Spanish £1.10 x-85-011031-
8
SHELVED AT 322.20946 CAM EXCEPT WHERE INDICATED:
Walton Ho.: 1 copy

CAMAIONE, D.N.
CONCEPTS IN KINESIOLOGY / by Richard Groves and David N.
Camaione. - 2nd ed. - Saunders, 1983 £13.95 0-03-062372-3
SHELVED AT 612.76 GRO EXCEPT WHERE INDICATED:
I.M. Marsh: 3 copies

CAMAIONE, D.N.
CONCEPTS IN KINESIOLOGY / by Groves,R. and Camaione,D.N. -
Saunders, 1975 £4.30 0-7216-4319-1
SHELVED AT 612.76 GRO EXCEPT WHERE INDICATED:
Byrom St.: 2 copies

CAMARA DE COMERCIO E INDUSTRIA DE MADRID
ECONOMIA ESPANOLA EN 1980 / by Camara De Comercio E Industria
De Madrid. - C.C.I.M., 1981 Spanish 84-5004321-2
SHELVED AT 330.946 CAM EXCEPT WHERE INDICATED:
Walton Ho.: 1 copy

CAMARDO, S.A.
BUILDING TOMORROW: THE MOBILE / MANUFACTURED HOUSING
INDUSTRY / by Bernhardt,A.G. , Camardo,S.A. and Zien,H.B. -
M.I.T. Press, 1980 ill. £33.25 x-85-018398-6
SHELVED AT 338.476908 BER EXCEPT WHERE INDICATED:
Clarence St.: 1 copy

CAMARGO, S.
CAMARGO / by Brett,G. - Signals, 1966 x-85-063556-9
Camargo,S.
SHELVED AT 730.92 CAM EXCEPT WHERE INDICATED:
Hope St.: 1 copy

CAMARGUE
CAMARGUE ET PAYS D ARLES / by Tondeur,F. - Nathan, 1968
French x-85-088172-1
SHELVED AT 914.49 TON EXCEPT WHERE INDICATED:
Walton Ho.: 1 copy

CAMARGUE
HORSES OF THE CAMARGUE / by Silvester,H. - Phaidon, 1976 ill.
£12.50 0-7148-1735-x
SHELVED AT 599.725 SIL EXCEPT WHERE INDICATED:
Hope St.: 1 copy

CAMATINI, E.
HEAT PUMPS AND THEIR CONTRIBUTION TO ENERGY CONSERVATION:
PROC. OF NATO ADVANCED STUDY INSTITUTE , LES ARCS , FRANCE ,
JUNE 16 - 27 1975 / ed. by Camatini,E. and Kester,T. -
Noordhoff, 1976 £19.58 90-2860056-6
SHELVED AT 621.4025 NAT EXCEPT WHERE INDICATED:
Byrom St.: 1 copy

CAMAZIAN, L.
HISTORY OF FRENCH LITERATURE / by Camazian,L. - O.U.P., 1967
x-85-083227-5
SHELVED AT 840.9 CAM EXCEPT WHERE INDICATED:
I.M. Marsh: 1 copy

CAMBA, J.
LA RANA VIAJERA / articulos humoristicos ; by Camba,J. - 1928
x-85-085731-6
SHELVED AT 867.6 CAM EXCEPT WHERE INDICATED:
Walton Ho. Reserve: 1 copy

CAMBELL, A.B.
GAS DYNAMICS / by Cambell,A.B. - Dover, 1958 x-85-036045-4
SHELVED AT 533.6 CAM EXCEPT WHERE INDICATED:
Byrom St.: 1 copy

CAMBERWELL
VICTORIAN SUBURB: A STUDY OF THE GROWTH OF CAMBERWELL / by
Dyos,H. - Leicester U.P., 1961 x-85-090542-6
SHELVED AT 942.16 DYO EXCEPT WHERE INDICATED:
Walton Ho. Reserve: 1 copy

Extract from Liverpool Polytechnic Library microfiche catalogue showing part of the alphabetical section which includes key word entries

Facing left: Extract from Cheshire Libraries microfiche catalogue. Cheshire uses partial Berghoeffer filing. Forenames are ignored and titles file alphabetically within surnames (See entries under BAYNES).
This is a multimedia catalogue. The section shown includes books, a computer program cassette (BBC MICRO . . .) and sound discs (BEACH BOYS)

Index frame of a microfiche card (Liverpool Polytechnic Library)

Filing

When a computer is used to produce a printed book or microform catalogue, the drudgery of 'filing' the entries in an alphabetic, numeric or alphanumeric order is removed since this can be done automatically.

As previously explained, each 'character' is allocated a particular 'value' within the machine and this facilitates sorting and merging. However, this does not solve all of the problems that will be encountered and library applications may require special arrangements in order to overcome:

1 Certain difficulties posed by a pre-determined character ranking order.

2 The fact that the computer cannot think like a human being.

Where (1) is concerned, for instance, if upper case letters

have less value than lower case letters (refer to page 75) then *The story of David Copperfield* and *The story of O* will file *before The story of aviation*, even though the latter comes *first* in alphabetical order.

With regard to (2), the computer could be instructed to 'ignore initial articles' and it would file *A tale of two cities* correctly under 'tale' but would it then file *A to Z hints for gardeners* under 'to hints for gardeners'? And how would it distinguish between *Die fledermaus* and *Die retouching*?

Several codes of filing rules, designed primarily for library applications and all compiled with the computer in mind, have been issued in recent years. Examples are the *ALA filing rules* (Chicago : American Library Association, 1980); the *BLAISE filing rules* (London : British Library, 1980); and the *Library of Congress filing rules* (Washington : LC, 1980).

All three of these publications adopt a 'word by word' (or 'nothing before something') rather than a 'letter by letter' (or 'all through') arrangement. The latter, unlike the former, ignores spaces and files alphabetically according to the letters contained in an entry regardless of whether or not they form complete words.

Word by word filing	*Letter by letter filing*
South	South
South Australia	Southampton
South pole	South Australia
Southampton	Southey
Southey	South pole

It is logical that the former should be chosen as the basic computer based method because a space usually has less value than any other character and this is therefore an easier system to program.

The rules also contain directions for dealing with other problems, for example:

1 Miscellaneous punctuation marks such as the dash, the hyphen and the diagonal slash.

　　All three sets of rules stipulate that the above should be given equal filing value to the space. ALA and LC add the full stop (period).

2 Initials, acronyms and abbreviations

　　All three codes, for instance, file abbreviations

exactly as written, so that the computer does not
have to work out what they mean.
3 Same word as author, title, subject, etc.
ALA arranges identical headings alphabetically by
the words following, while BLAISE and LC prefer
'classified' groupings.

Rules for computer filing can be helpful for offline catalogue production but, as the last example above illustrates,
there are still differences of opinion and a lack of international agreement as to how such filing should be done.
Further, commercially available database management
packages may have in-built sorting routines which follow
different directions.

Online access catalogues

When accessing the catalogue online, the results of a search
will either (a) be displayed on the vdu screen or (b) output to
a printer. The former may be the only facility available or,
alternatively, the initial search results may be viewed on the
screen and, when a satisfactory result has been obtained, a
print-out of the relevant entry or entries may be requested.
The latter is obviously desirable. 'The ability to print catalog
records is a feature unique to online catalogs — a feature
much appreciated by library patrons.'[1] There may, of course,
be a number of records that satisfy a particular search criteria.
This means, in effect, that it may be possible to print out
selective bibliographies and booklists in hard copy.

The formats chosen for screen display and print-out will
often vary, as a format that is suitable for one may not be
suitable for the other. Systems will sometimes make allowance
for this and permit different formats to be set up for different
purposes. Salmon concludes that 'Display formats should
probably include an 'index' format, with one or two lines,
and a 'brief' format. A full bibliographic format is also
desirable. Less clear, however, is whether a MARC format is
really needed.'[2]

Some of the criteria, eg layout, spacing, etc, already
discussed in relation to offline are also relevant to online.

1 Printing and the online catalog / Bennett J. Price *Information technology and libraries* 3 (1) March 1984 15-20
2 Characteristics of online public catalogs / Stephen R. Salmon *Library
resources and technical services* 27 (1) January/March 1983 36-67

The screen should not be overcrowded; entries, if there is more than one displayed at a time, should be clearly distinguishable and particular elements within the entry should be identifiable.

Some questions which might be asked in connection with the above are:

1 Is a single entry only to be displayed at any one time?
2 If not, how are the entries to be separated?
3 How much detail is to be included in a displayed entry?
4 Is a choice of level of detail to be provided?
5 Is a narrative, paragraph type display (as on a catalogue card) to be used or is a tabular form to be preferred?
6 If a tabular form is to be used, are the various elements to be labelled?

As online catalogues have become more prevalent, 'Many librarians have urged catalog planners and designers to retain the traditional main entry card format. These librarians feel that this format should at least be included among the alternatives available to the user, if not the 'standard' format in an online catalog'.[1] But, as Hildreth, from whom this quote is taken, points out, this opinion 'though popular, is not universally shared'[2] and many librarians see the traditional format as unsuitable in an online context. Recent studies recognize the importance of display format design and appear to indicate that tabular or labelled formats (see page 96) are preferred to traditional or narrative layouts (see page 85) by the user.[3] Hard copy print-out may allow a more 'conventional' catalogue type layout and will probably not require labels for field names.

Not all online catalogues are *public* catalogues. An often encountered combination, for instance, will be an online access facility for the library staff and an offline microfiche catalogue for the library user. The screen display formats required by cataloguing staff may be not at all suitable for public consumption. Too much detail could be present and field 'names' might be simply MARC tags which would be somewhat meaningless to the layman.

An online public access catalogue is, however, obviously

1 *Online public access catalogs : the user interface* / Charles R. Hildreth.
 — OCLC, 1982 145
2 *ibid.*
3 *ibid. 146-147*

```
TITLE    INFORMATION HANDLING IN MUSEUMS
AUTHOR   ORNA, ELIZABETH ; PETTITT, CHARLES
PUBL     BINGLEY
DATE     1980
CLASS    069
```

```
PRESS RETURN FOR NEXT RECORD OR M FOR MENU   ?
```

```
TITLE    INTRODUCTION TO MUSEUM WORK
AUTHOR   BURCAW, G. ELLIS
EDN      2ND ED
PUBL     AMERICAN ASSOCIATION FOR STATE AND LOCAL HISTORY
DATE     1975
CLASS    069
```

```
PRESS RETURN FOR NEXT RECORD OR M FOR MENU   ?
```

```
TITLE    MUSEUMS AND HOW TO USE THEM
AUTHOR   ALEXANDER, EUGENIE
PUBL     BATSFORD
DATE     1974
CLASS    069
```

```
LISTING IS NOW COMPLETE

PRESS RETURN FOR MENU   ?
```

Simple screen display format, which permits multiple entries to be displayed simultaneously, as used for teaching purposes by Liverpool Polytechnic School of Librarianship and Information Studies. Other fields, eg ISBN, may be present in the record, and searchable, but can be suppressed in the display

preferable — 'The online catalog is a far more powerful instrument than any of its predecessors.'[1] How, therefore, is it viewed by the user? In 1981, the Council on Library

1 The online catalog revolution / Frederick G. Kilgour *Library journal* 109 (3) February 15 1984 319-321

```
Screen 1 of 2
NO HOLDINGS IN EUN - FOR HOLDINGS ENTER dh DEPRESS DISPLAY RECD SEND
OCLC: 4163918      Rec stat: n Entrd: 780804     Used: 831206
Type: a Bib lvl: m Govt pub:   Lang:   ita Source:   Illus: a
Repr:   Enc lvl:   Conf pub: 0 Ctry: it Dat tp: s M/F/B: 10
Indx: 0 Mod rec:   Festschr: 0 Cont: b
Desc: P Int lvl:   Dates: 1976,
 1 010     78-360027
 2 040     DLC lc DLC
 3 015     It78-Feb
 4 020     lc L2800
 5 043     e-it---
 6 050  0  DG55.L6 lb S77
 7 092     lb
 8 049     EUNN
 9 100 20  Struffolino Albricci, Anna, ld 1938-
10 245 10  Lombardia romana : lb le citt'a / lc Anna Struffolino Albricci.
11 250     1. ed.
12 260  0  Milano : lb Arte lombarda, lc 1976.
13 300     83 p. ; lb ill. ; lc 22 cm.
14 440  0  Taccuini di Arte lombarda ; lv 1
15 504     Bibliography: p. 76-77.
16 651  0  Lombardy lx Antiquities, Roman.
17 650  0  Cities and towns lz Italy lz Lombardy.
```

OCLC screen format display. Note the tags, indicators and subfield codes of the MARC format. A full MARC display could run to several screens

Resources provided the funding to enable five organizations in the US (J. Matthews & Associates, Library of Congress, Online Computer Library Centre Inc (OCLC), the Research Libraries Group (RLG), and the University of California's Division of Library Automation to conduct a study of library users and online public access catalogues. Results began to flow from this massive study in mid-1982[1] and the full report was published in mid-1983.[2] One of the major findings was that there is great user satisfaction with this form of catalogue; 94% of all users in the survey preferred the online catalogue to the card catalogue. (The main transition in the US has been from card direct to online, the COM catalogue being largely bi-passed. This contrasts sharply with the position in the UK.) One feature of other physical forms of catalogue which users apparently like to see in the online form is browsability, ie a facility for scanning a number of entries at once (see below).

Not only does the public access catalogue overcome the problems of the printed book and COM forms, eg lack of currency, filing difficulties, multiple sequences, etc, but it offers other advantages. The following is a list of the possibilities as seen by the developers of the University of California's MELVYL system:[3]

1 It could be easily updated — in real time or overnight — and hence would be much more up to date.
2 It could be more accurate because corrections and changes could be made easily and immediately.
3 It would allow faster catalogue searching for the user because the computer could do the searching and display the results within a few seconds.
4 It could provide for searching under multiple terms, or keywords, not just the initial words of the headings chosen in the cataloguing process.

1 *See, for example,* The CLR public online catalog study: an overview / Douglas Ferguson *et al. Information technology and libraries* 1 (2) June 1982 84-97
2 *Using online catalogs : a nationwide survey* / edited by Joseph R. Matthews, Gary S. Lawrence and Douglas Ferguson. — Neal-Schuman, 1983
3 In-depth : University of California MELVYL *Information technology and libraries* 1 (4) December 1982 351-371 *and* 2 (1) March 1983 58-115

5 It could allow combinations of terms or keywords to limit or define a search more precisely.

6 The interactive nature of an online system could make it easier to provide guidance to the user in finding and locating material.

7 The filing rule problems would be greatly lessened, both for librarians and users, because the computer would both store and retrieve all the information.

8 A variety of display formats could be used (and chosen) by the user.

9 The terminals used for the online catalogue could be used to provide access to other databases, or terminals already in use for other purposes could be used to access the union catalogue.

'In contrast with the existing card catalogs on most of the campuses, an online catalog could also be much more complete; it could display several entries at once, on the same screen, to facilitate browsing; it could be more portable (that is, terminals could be installed at various locations on campus, even in dormitories and offices); and the terminals would not only occupy less space but would allow greater flexibility in providing space for them.'

No wonder that the final University plan, then, 'strongly endorsed the online catalog' as the form of the new proposed system.

There is one problem associated with the online catalogue, of course, and that is that, being machine-based, it could break down. A library may consider it necessary to have a spare processor available or to maintain some form of back-up catalogue in hard copy or COM. The provision of a hard copy back-up would obviously be expensive and time consuming and hardly cost beneficial. However, it may well be, as Perry suggests, that 'producing some kind of COM catalogue on an infrequent basis is a very good idea.'[1]

Among the principles that served to guide the developers of the MELVYL system were that it should be user-friendly and that it should have a syndetic structure that was transparent to the user. Thus, for example, the authority control

1 The implementation of an online public catalogue / Niall Perry *In Introducing the online catalogue : papers based on seminars held in 1983* / edited by Alan Seal. — Bath University Library Centre for Catalogue Research, 1984 43

subsystem would automatically retrieve the works of an author through various forms of the name, so that the user need not be familiar with cataloguing practice to do a thorough search.

One very interesting point in relation to online catalogues and catalogue use surveys is that it now becomes possible to examine the way in which the reader approaches and uses the catalogue without the reader being aware that he is being observed, ie by using the inbuilt capabilities of the machine. Clearly this makes for a more realistic and unbiased analysis. It could be ascertained, for instance, how many searches had been undertaken for a known item and how many for a subject.

Online catalogues will be considered further from the search point of view in a later section.

```
27   University of Sussex 19-06-84 14:36

AUTHOR:   Campbell,T

TITLE:    Seven Theories of Human Society : The Theories of Aristotle, Hobbes, A
dam Smith, Marx, Durkheim, Weber and Alfred Schutz

IMPRINT:  Clarendon P.   1981
          Number of copies owned by the Library or on order:  5

Book no.    Location Shelfmark        Loan category &  Status

562371 4    MAIN     HB 400 Cam       LONG    Out; due 15-10-84
581126 9    SHORT    HB 400 Cam       SHORT   Out; due 21-06-84
581127 X    RES      HB 400 Cam       RES     Ask in Reserve
586020 2    ORDER                     SHORT   On order
586021 3    ORDER                     SHORT   On order

Choose from this list, enter here: █           Then press `SEND´.
F - go Forwards (seeing 5 records)     E - see choice of search types; or use
B - go Backwards                           search letter if you know it (eg T)
Z - see next record only,in this format
S - input new QUICK-KEY for searching  X - go back to main selection menu
```

University of Sussex Library (UK). Online screen format response to book query. This is a Geac-based system

```
┌──────────────────────────────────────────────────────────────────┐
│    8 SUSSEX UNIVERSITY LIBRARY 28-09-83   DISPLAY: full / all  ACCESS LEVEL: 0 │
│  FUNCTION: BIBLIOGRAPHIC QUERY / UPDATE   TIME: 14:45      PRESS 'HLP' FOR HELP │
│                                                                    │
│  COMMAND: DISP SUBCOMMAND:      SEARCH TYPE:  BROWSE KEY:A  DIRECTION:+  AMT:01 │
│  SEARCH STRING: /LAANIMAG                                           │
│                                                                    │
│  CLASS:    PK 82519 Laa                                            │
│  AUTHOR(S):Laane,TV fsMeyer,CF                                     │
│                                                                    │
│  TITLE(S): Imagery in Conrad Ferdinand Meyer's prose works : form, motifs, and fu │
│  nctions fsGermanic studies in America fv47                        │
│                                                                    │
│  IMPRINT: Lang flBerne fd1983                                      │
│  ISBN:    3261032510                                               │
│  SPEC.NAME:                                                        │
│                                                                    │
│  STF.NOTE:                                                         │
│                                                                    │
│  PUB.NOTE:                                                         │
│  Total copies in stock or on order: 2                             │
│                                                                    │
│  Level: GGRA   T.Srce: DB   Lang: E        ADDed: 17-03-83   UPDated: 12-05-83 │
│                                                                    │
│  Updpnt: Y    Spare : SPARE  Holds since 03-83: 0                 │
└──────────────────────────────────────────────────────────────────┘
```

Source record:

Name entries:

    Laane, T.V.   PK 82519 Laa
      Imagery in Conrad Ferdinand Meyer's prose works : form,
      motifs, and functions / Laane, T.V. - Lang, Berne, 1983
      (Germanic studies in America ; 47)
      1 Long   (t574476-4)
      (On order/in process: 1 Short)

    Meyer, C.F. (Subject)   PK 82519 Laa
      Imagery in Conrad Ferdinand Meyer's prose works : form,
      motifs, and functions / Laane, T.V. - Lang, Berne, 1983
      (Germanic studies in America ; 47)
      1 Long   (t574476-4)
      (On order/in process: 1 Short)

(Series and) Title entries:

    Germanic studies in America   PK 82519 Laa
      Imagery in Conrad Ferdinand Meyer's prose works : form,
      motifs, and functions / Laane, T.V. - Lang, Berne, 1983
      (Germanic studies in America ; 47)
      1 Long   (t574476-4)
      (On order/in process: 1 Short)

    Imagery in Conrad Ferdinand Meyer's,...   PK 82519 Laa
      Imagery in Conrad Ferdinand Meyer's prose works : form,
      motifs, and functions / Laane, T.V. - Lang, Berne, 1983
      (Germanic studies in America ; 47)
      1 Long   (t574476-4)
      (On order/in process: 1 Short)

An entry with a summary of usage and acquisitions data:

    Laane, T.V.   PK 82519 Laa
      Imagery in Conrad Ferdinand Meyer's prose works : form,
      motifs, and functions / Laane, T.V. - Lang, Berne, 1983
      (Germanic studies in America ; 47)
      1 Long   (t574476-4)
      (On order/in process: 1 Short)
      (Added entry Meyer, C.F.)
      T.Srce DB   Level GGRA
      574476-4 MAIN LONG   --- --- --- --- --- 1L   1 * 05-83   2
      588976-3 ORDER SHORT --- --- --- --- ---   0 *   0
      Accn   d acc price fd d avl loc   del/ms d d/m
      574476-4 03-83 £ 21.19 40 05-83 MAIN In stk
      588976-3   Unknown ?   ORDER

University of Sussex Library. Examples of offline output formats — produced by batch mode report generator and output on printer or magnetic tape for COM

User: DISPLAY REVIEW or DISPLAY 1-13 REVIEW or DISPLAY ALL REVIEW
MELVYL:

Search request: FIND SU IMAGINATION CHILDREN
Search result: 13 records at UC libraries

    1. COBB, Edith, 1895-1977.   The ecology of imagination in... 1977
    2. DAVIDSON, Audrey, 1916-   Phantasy in childhood, by Audrey... 1952
    3. The Development of children's imaginative writing / edited by Helen... 1983
    4. The Development of children's imaginative writing / edited by Helen... 1984
    5. The Development of children's imaginative writing / edited by Helen... 1984
    6. The Development of children's imaginative writing / edited by Helen... 1984
    7. FEIN, Greta G.   Cognitive and social dimensions of... 1976
    8. GRIFFITHS, Ruth.   A study of imagination in early... 1970
    9. JEAN, Georges.   Bachelard, l'enfance et la... 1983
   10. PIAGET, Jean, 1896-   Mental imagery in the child; a... 1971
   11. PRUYSER, Paul W.   The play of the imagination :... 1983
   12. SINGER, Dorothy G.   Partners in play ; a step-by-step... 1977
   13. SINGER, Jerome L.   Television, imagination, and... 1981

User: DISPLAY 10 SHORT or DISPLAY 10 BRIEF
MELVYL:

Search request: FIND SU IMAGINATION CHILDREN
Search result: 13 records at UC libraries

10. Piaget, Jean, 1896-
    Mental imagery in the child; a study of the development of imaginal
    representation [by] Jean Piaget and Barbel Inhelder, in collaboration with
    M. Bovet [and others] Translated from the French by P. A. Chilton.
    New York, Basic Books [1971]
       UCD   HealthSci WS105 P4713
       UCI   Main Lib BF723.15 P513
       UCSC   McHenry   BF723.15P513

User: DISPLAY 10 LONG
MELVYL:

Search request: FIND SU IMAGINATION CHILDREN
Search result: 13 records at UC libraries

10.
Author: Piaget, Jean, 1896-
Uniform title: L'Image mentale chez l'enfant. English.
Title: Mental imagery in the child; a study of the development of
                 imaginal representation [by] Jean Piaget and Barbel Inhelder,
                 in collaboration with M. Bovet [and others] Translated from
                 the French by P. A. Chilton. New York, Basic Books [1971]
                 xix, 396 p. illus. 24 cm.

Notes: Translation of L'Image mentale chez l'enfant.
                 Includes bibliographical references.

Subjects: Child psychology.
                 Imagination -- in infancy & childhood.
                 Perception -- in infancy & childhood.

Other entries: Inhelder, Barbel, joint author.

Call numbers: UCD   HealthSci WS105 P4713 (CU-AM)
                 UCI   Main Lib BF723.15 P513 (CU-I)
                 UCSC   McHenry   BF723.15P513 (CU-SC)

University of California MELVYL system. Examples of REVIEW, BRIEF and LONG screen formats

Chapter Seven

Searching

If the physical form of output is in hard copy, eg card or printed book format, then the search methodology for the computer produced catalogue will be exactly the same as when the catalogue is produced in some other way. 'Conventional' classified and dictionary arrangements may be used as illustrated below.

A similar situation exists where output is via microform, which is, in effect, a printed form very much reduced in size. However, the size factor is important because, as previously indicated, it makes possible the provision of additional access points, which with computer production, can quite easily be generated.

Apart from classified and dictionary formats, the computer can be used to produce other 'inner' forms of catalogues and indexes. A keyword from title list, for instance, may require no intellectual effort to produce. Entries are automatically generated for all title words apart from those on 'stoplists'. Various types of subject index are also very often computer produced. Some examples will be found on the following pages.

Whilst it is still necessary, at this moment in time, to consider such approaches as those illustrated below, two facts can be stated with some certainty:

1 The printed book, card or microform computer produced catalogues are interim forms only. All will eventually be replaced by online systems.

2 Traditional classified/dictionary arrangements, in the context of online access, are redundant. Online searching offers much more flexible and exciting possibilities.

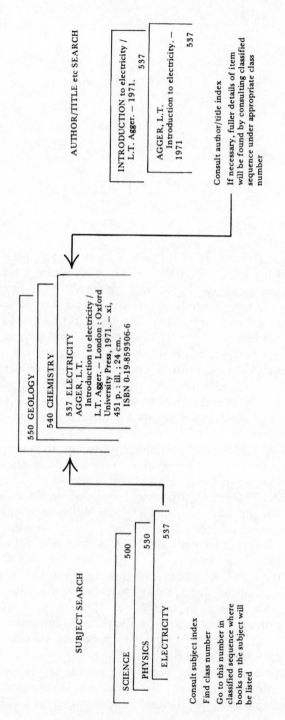

Searching in the classified catalogue

SCIENCE
see also
PHYSICS

PHYSICS
see also
ELECTRICITY

INTRODUCTION to electricity /
L.T. Agger. — 1971.
537

ELECTRICITY
AGGER, L.T.
    Introduction to electricity. —
1971.
537

AGGER, L.T.
    Introduction to electricity /
L.T. Agger. — London : Oxford
University Press, 1971. — xi,
451 p. : ill. ; 24 cm.
    ISBN 0-19-859306-6
537

THOR/TITLE/SUBJECT
SEARCH

nsult alphabetical sequence

necessary, fuller details of an
n will be found under 'main'
ry, which is usually that for
ponsible person or body

ferences guide user between headings

te:
it' entry type catalogues provide
milar amount of detail in all
ries
ne catalogues separate subject
m other entries to form a
ided' catalogue

Searching in the dictionary catalogue

INTRODUCTION to electricity /
L.T. Agger. — 1971.
537

ELECTRICITY
AGGER, L.T.
    Introduction to electricity. —
1971.
537

AGGER, L.T.
    Introduction to electricity. —
1971.
537

Author/title section
of classified catalogue
'enriched' by keyword
from title entries
to form an alphabetical
catalogue/index

Searching in the classified catalogue

```
          FOTHERINGHAM : AMERICAN GOVERNMENT AND POLITICS          [320.473
   FALKUS : THE SPANISH   ARMADA                                   [942.05
            PUNNETT :   BRITISH GOVERNMENT AND POLITICS            [320.442
            CLIFTON :   BUSINESS DATA SYSTEMS                      [658.4032
      CLIFTON : BUSINESS   DATA SYSTEMS                            [658.4032
         WOOD : INSHORE   DINGHY FISHING                           [799.1
               FALKUS : THE SPANISH ARMADA                         [942.05
   WOOD : INSHORE DINGHY   FISHING                                 [799.1
FOTHERINGHAM : AMERICAN GOVERNMENT AND POLITICS                    [320.473
   FOTHERINGHAM : AMERICAN   GOVERNMENT AND POLITICS               [320.473
        PUNNETT : BRITISH   GOVERNMENT AND POLITICS                [320.442
              WOOD :   INSHORE DINGHY FISHING                      [799.1
FOTHERINGHAM : AMERICAN GOVERNMENT AND   POLITICS                  [320.473
   PUNNETT : BRITISH GOVERNMENT AND   POLITICS                     [320.442
        PUNNETT : BRITISH GOVERNMENT AND POLITICS                  [320.442
           FALKUS : THE   SPANISH ARMADA                           [942.05
      CLIFTON : BUSINESS DATA   SYSTEMS                            [658.4032
                WOOD : INSHORE DINGHY FISHING'                     [799.1
```

AKWIC (Author and Key Word In Context) computer produced index (generated, in this instance, by means of a program written by G B Moersdorf at Ohio State University). Entries under unwanted key words, eg 'The', 'And', etc are automatically suppressed by means of a 'stoplist'

Control No.	Subject	Classmark
S1887040 *	CATHOLICISM	282
S1928543 *	CAUSATION	122
S2508576 *	CAUSATION: LAW	340.11
S1878696 *	CAVES: GEOMORPHOLOGY	551.44
S1883467 *	: GEOMORPHOLOGY: BIBLIOGRAPHIES	016.55144
S1549892 *	CAVITATION: HYDRODYNAMICS: PHYSICS	532.528
S1891739 *	CEEFAX: DATA TRANSMISSION: TELEVISION: ELECTRICAL ENGINEERING	621.397
S155907X *	CEILINGS: ARCHITECTURAL CONSTRUCTION	721.7
S1558804 *	: BUILDING	690.17
S1552693 *	CELESTIAL MECHANICS: ASTRONOMY	521.1
S1563679 *	CELL BIOLOGY	576.3
S1533563 *	CELL DIFFERENTIATION: GENETIC CONTROL: MOLECULAR GENETICS: BIOLOGY	577.218
S1558655 *	CELL DIVISION: BIOLOGY	576.35
S1546149 *	CELL INTERACTIONS: CYTOLOGY: BIOLOGY	576.52
S1572135 *	CELL METABOLISM: BIOLOGY	576.34
S1560557 *	CELL MORPHOLOGY: BIOLOGY	576.31
S1561060 *	CELL MOTILITY: BIOLOGY	576.32
S1572371 *	CELL NUTRITION: BIOLOGY	576.34
S1558402 *	CELLS: ALGAE: BOTANY	589.30487
S1572365 *	: BIOLOGY	576.3
	BOTANY	
S1546273 *	: BOTANY	581.17
S1558052 *	: FUNGI: BOTANY	589.20487
S155913X *	CELLULAR DIFFERENTIATION: DEVELOPMENTAL BIOLOGY	576.5
S1874132 *	CELLULAR MEMBRANES SEE MEMBRANES	
S1546267 *	CELLULAR RECOGNITION: CYTOLOGY: BIOLOGY	576.52
S1893916 *	CELLULOSE: ORGANIC CHEMISTRY	547.4588
S1883740 *	CELTIC BRITAIN: HISTORY	936.102
S250688X *	CELTIC LANGUAGES	491.6
S1535045 *	CELTIC REGIONS: ANCIENT HISTORY	936.4
S1534270 *	CELTS: GREAT BRITAIN: ART METALWORK	739.09361
S1552902 *	CENOZOIC PALAEONTOLOGY	560.178
S156578X *	CENOZOIC STRATIGRAPHY: GEOLOGY	551.78
S192496X *	CENSORSHIP: BOOKS	098.1
S1871553 *	: LAW	344.0531
S1544742 *	: LIBRARY STOCK	025.213
S1886135 *	: SOCIAL ASPECTS	363.31
S2509831 *	: TELEVISION	791.45
S1881439 *	CENSUS RESEARCH	312.072
S1529748 *	CENTRAL ADMINISTRATION: MILITARY SCIENCE	355.6

Extract from a laser printed subject index generated for the Polytechnic of North London by BLCMP Library Services Ltd. It is to the Polytechnic's requirements; in other circumstances the display could be rearranged, eg the control numbers suppressed and the classmark/subject string inverted

Beasts *See* Animals
Beauty
  See also
    Aesthetics
Beauty care
  Science — *Questions & answers* — *For beauty care*
                    502′.46467

Beauty care. Women
  Use of natural food   646.7′2
Bedford motor coaches
  Bedford VAL motor coaches, *to 1983*   629.2′2233
Bedfordshire lace
  Making — *Manuals*   746.2′22
Bedrooms. Residences
  Interior design   747.7′7

    Food
      See also
        Cakes
        Carob
        Cookery
        Diet
        Edible plants
        Fruit. Food
        Honey
        Lemons
        Meals
        Meat
        Natural food
        Nutrition
        Pizzas
        Pulses. Vegetables
        Sauces

    Nations *See* States
    Nativity. Jesus Christ
      — *Stories for children*   232.9′21
      Historicity   232.7′21
    Natural environment. Great Britain
      — *Correspondence, diaries, etc.*   508.41
    Natural food
      See also
        Dishes using natural food
    Natural food
      Use in beauty care of women   646.7′2
    Natural gas deposits. North Sea
      Natural gas deposits & petroleum deposits
                  553.2′8′0916336

    Women
      — *Quotations*   305.4
      Beauty care. Use of natural food 646.7′2
      Benzodiazepines. Action — *For women* 615′.7882
      Great Britain. Personal finance — *For women*
                  332.024′042′0941
      Interpersonal relationships with men — *Quotations* —
        Collections   305.3
      Miscarriages   618.3′92
      Personal adjustment to separation & divorce — *Manuals*
                  306.8′9′088042
      Personal finance — *For women* 332.024′042
      Pregnancy — *For children*   618.2
      Pregnancy & childbirth — *Manuals* — *For mothers*
                  618.2′00240431

Computer produced PRECIS index entries from the May 1984 British national bibliography. Note the degree of articulation and the way in which the context of the subject is preserved at each entry point. An open-ended controlled vocabulary automatically links related or synonymous terms

PRESTRESSED CONCRETE STRUCTURAL COMPONENTS : DESIGN •624.183412• AND 624.1834
PRESTRESSED CONCRETE STRUCTURES : DEMOLITION 624.183412
PRESTRESSED CONCRETE STRUCTURES : DESIGN •624.183412• AND 624.1834
PRESTRESSED MASONRY : CONSTRUCTION MATERIALS 624.183
PRESTRESSED MICROCONCRETE MODELS : STRUCTURAL ENGINEERING : 624.1834
    DESIGN : USE : OF
PRESTRESSING STEEL : CONSTRUCTION MATERIALS 624.1821
PRESTRESSING STEEL : CONSTRUCTION MATERIALS : TESTING 624.1821
PRESUPPOSITIONS : STATEMENTS, IMPLICATIONS : SEMANTICS 149.94
PRESYNAPTIC RECEPTORS : MAMMALS 599.0188
PREVENTION OF TERRORISM (TEMPORARY PROVISIONS) ACT 1974 : 345.410231
    TERRORISM : PREVENTION : GREAT BRITAIN : LAW
PREVENTIVE MAINTENANCE 658.202
PREVENTIVE MEDICINE 614.44
PREVENTIVE MEDICINE : GREAT BRITAIN 614.440941
PREVENTIVE MEDICINE : LONDON 614.4409421
PREVENTIVE MEDICINE : SCREENING 614.44
PREVENTIVE MEDICINE SEE ALSO IMMUNISATION
PRICE MANAGEMENT : PURCHASING : INDUSTRIES 658.72
PRICE MARKING (BARGAIN OFFERS) ORDER 1979 : 344.10383
    TRADE DESCRIPTIONS ACT 1968 : GREAT BRITAIN : LAW :
    AMENDMENT PROPOSALS
PRICE MARKING (BARGAIN OFFERS) ORDERS 1979 : CRITICAL STUDIES 344.10383
PRICE, RICHARD : MORAL PHILOSOPHY : THEORIES 171.6
PRICE-LEVEL ACCOUNTING •657.48• AND 657.3
PRICE-LEVEL ACCOUNTING : LOCAL AUTHORITIES : GREAT BRITAIN 352.170941
PRICES : ACADEMIC BOOKS 338.43002
PRICES : ACETYLENES 338.4366585
PRICES : ADJUSTMENT : FORMULAE : BUILDINGS : CONSTRUCTION : 692.5
    CONTRACTS
PRICES : ADVERTISING : EFFECTS : ON 338.52

Extract from Lancashire Polytechnic's (UK) 'PRECIS style' subject index which is currently on microfiche. When two classification numbers are displayed with an entry the first is the 19th ed Dewey decimal classification number and the second is the 18th ed number. (The production of this index is described in: The provision of a subject index at Preston Polytechnic Library and Learning Resources Service : use of an adaptation of PRECIS at Preston Polytechnic / Frances Hendrix Program 15 (2) April 1981 73-90)

Searching in the online catalogue

Essentially, an online catalogue will feature one of three basic approaches for searching: *menu, command* or *free text.*

The *menu* approach provides the user with a series of options which will be displayed on the screen of the vdu, eg:

```
DO YOU WISH TO SEARCH UNDER
    1  AUTHOR
    2  TITLE
    3  SUBJECT
ENTER APPROPRIATE NUMBER AND
    THEN PRESS RETURN KEY
```

A mnemonic feature can be introduced by replacing the numbers with letters, eg:

```
A  AUTHOR
T  TITLE
S  SUBJECT
```

After the user has selected an option more guidance may be given, for example, if option 'A' is chosen:

```
ENTER THE AUTHOR THAT YOU REQUIRE
SURNAME FIRST FOLLOWED BY A SPACE
AND THEN THE INITIALS EXCLUDING
PUNCTUATION MARKS
```

Care must be taken where the form of name is concerned. As previously noted, if an author is indexed as SMITH, JOHN, a search on SMITH JOHN will fail. The user must be instructed as to the correct format.

Although the menu approach could be described as 'user-friendly', it can become somewhat slow and tedious once one is familiar with search methodology, especially if a series of menus and sub-menus, which may be irrelevant to the particular enquiry, have to be worked through.

```
  27  University of Sussex 19-06-84 14:35
PUBLIC QUERY:  BOOK & BORROWING QUERIES

Enter either

   1 - to look for a book or a periodical
   or
   2 - to display information about
       your own borrowing

then press the red `SEND´ key.
     ENTER: █
```

1 selected

```
  27   University of Sussex 19-06-84 14:36
               ONLINE CATALOGUE

   Q - QUICK search - 8 key taps only!
   A - AUTHOR or NAME search
   W - SPECIFIC NAME search
   T - TITLE search (inc. periodicals)
   K - KEYWORD-IN-TITLE search
   C - CLASSMARK search
   X - Go back to main selection menu
Choose a letter, type it here:█
            then tap the red SEND key
```

University of Sussex Library's online catalogue top level menus

A method rather different to that described above but one which still might be considered a 'menu' type of approach is the 'form filling' technique where the complete record format is displayed on the screen. The user selects the required option by moving the cursor to the relevant field and then typing in the search term:

```
AUTHOR_SURNAME: .TROMBETTA. . . . . . . . . . . . . . . . . . .
AUTHOR_INITIALS (EXCLUDE PUNCTUATION AND SPACES): .M . .
TITLE . . . . . . . . . . . . . . . . . . . . . . . . . . . . . . . . . . .
. . . . . . . . . . . . . . . . . . . . . . . . . . . . . . . . . . . . . . .
PUBLISHER: . . . . . . . . . . . . . . . . . . . . . . . . . DATE: . . . .
SUBJECT: . . . . . . . . . . . . . . . . . . . . . . . . . . . . . . . . .
CLASS: . . . . . . . . . . . . . . . . . . . . . . . . . . . . . . . . . . .
        ENTER REQUIRED SEARCH TERM(S) IN APPROPRIATE
                     FIELD AND PRESS SEND
```

When the required record has been retrieved, the computer will display it on the screen using the same format:

```
AUTHOR_SURNAME: TROMBETTA
AUTHOR_INITIALS: M
TITLE: BASIC FOR STUDENTS : WITH APPLICATIONS

PUBLISHER: ADDISON-WESLEY                    DATE: 1981
SUBJECT: BASIC (COMPUTER PROGRAM LANGUAGE)
CLASS: HF5548.5.B3T76
```

```
    Commence search  . . . . . . .   S
    Consult subject index  . . . . . .  I
    List classification . . . . . . . .   C
    List author/title codes  . . . . .   A
    Need help . . . . . . . . . . .   H
    Quit  . . . . . . . . . . . . . .   Q

        Press appropriate key :
```

```
            Enter search code(s)
          (press RETURN to skip)
        Classification : . . . . . . . . . . . . . . . . . . . .
        Author/title code(s): . . . . . . . .  . . . . . . . .  . . . . . . . .
                              . . . . . . . .  . . . . . . . .  . . . . . . . .
        Type : . . . . . . . . . .
```

*User's menu and enquiry screen from LIBRARIAN (above)
and (below) sample entries from the University of Buckingham
Library subject index produced using this package. This is an
online subject index which must be consulted before a search
can be made for a classification number. (See also page 45.)*

```
    LAW REFORM                      340.3
    LAW OF PHYSICS                  530.01
    LAWYERS                         340.023
    LEAGUE OF NATIONS:LAW           341.22
    LEGISLATURES:POL SCI            328
    LIBERAL PARTY:GB                324.24106
    LIBRARIANSHIP                   02
    LINCOLN'S INN                   340.0941
    LITERATURE                      8
    LOCAL GOVERNMENT                352
    MACROECONOMIC POLICY            339.5
    MACROECONOMICS                  339
    MAINTENANCE:TAX LAW:GB          343.410524
    MANAGEMENT (GENERAL)            658
    MANAGEMENT (EXECUTIVE)          658.4
    MARKETING:BUSINESS              658.8
    MATHEMATICAL ECONOMICS          330.1543
    MATHEMATICS                     51
    MEDIATION:INTERNAT LAW          341.52
    MICROECONOMICS                  338.5
    MINORITY GROUPS:SOCIOLOGY       305.8
    MONEY:FINANCIAL ECONOMICS       332.4
```

```
You may search for books in one of two ways:

    by AUTHOR and/or TITLE
    or by SUBJECT.
-----------------------------------------------------------------------------------
Type the letter you want below or type HELP,   then press RETURN.
   A -  AUTHOR/TITLE search.
   S -  SUBJECT search.

->
```

University of California MELVYL system. LOOKUP search prompt screen (above)

and

Explanation display (below) if user types HELP instead of making a search selection

```
You must now choose the type of search that you want MELVYL to perform.

Choose AUTHOR/TITLE search if you know the author and/or the title of the book
you want to find.  MELVYL will ask you for the author's name,  and  for  words
from  the title.  You need not know the author's entire name, and you need not
know the full title.  You can find books knowing the author only, or the title
only.

Choose SUBJECT search if you are looking for books on a particular topic.  You
will be asked to type words that describe your topic.  MELVYL will find  books
containing those words in either the title or the subject headings.
-----------------------------------------------------------------------------------
Type the letter you want below,  then press RETURN.
   A - AUTHOR/TITLE search.
   S - SUBJECT search.

->
```

With the *command* approach, the user types instructions to the computer, eg:

FIND AUTHOR SHAKESPEARE

Unfortunately, there is no consistency or standardization of command languages and there may well be no explanation of the available commands given on the screen. The user must obtain these from some other source, eg an adjacent explanatory chart, leaflet, or manual.

Some catalogues do incorporate screen explanation, eg:

TO SEARCH FOR AN AUTHOR TYPE
  FIND AUTHOR
FOLLOWED BY THE AUTHOR'S SURNAME, E.G.
  FIND AUTHOR SALTER

It is possible to abbreviate commands in many systems, eg:

F A SALTER

or S/n/020107611X

where S means 'search for' and 'n' indicates 'number'.

The command mode can become quite complex and the user may have to be provided with detailed instructions. Simple commands such as FIND may be quite easy to understand but others, eg BACKUP (to return to a previous search result after a modification) or BROWSE (to review the access terms in the indexes that can be searched) are more difficult. In addition, facilities such as 'stringsearching' could be available. An example would be:

FIND TITLE CONTAINS TREES

or F T CT TREES

which would find any title which contained the term 'trees'. Stringsearching is a very useful facility. It enables a search to be made for a string of characters which is contained within a larger string. One form is the 'keyword' from title type of search shown above but it is also possible to search the whole of a record as in free text searching.

Quick Guide   1

This summary is a quick reference guide. Please refer to the Users' Guide that follows for full instructions.

Command words below are capitalized. When there is a choice of command words, they have been listed consecutively, separated by slashes (/).

ALL words in the command language, except index names, can be abbreviated to 3 letters. FIND, DISPLAY, and HELP can be abbreviated to 1 letter.

HELP

HELP—to request assistance at any time

HELP [term]—to request information about terms relating to the catalog
  e.g., HELP DISPLAY

FIND (Search)

New search

FIND [index] [keyword(s)] AND/OR/AND NOT [index] [keyword(s)]. . .
  Indexes:

PA (Personal author)   UT (Uniform title)
CA (Corporate author)   SE (Series)
TI (Title)   SU (Subject)

Enter personal names in inverted order (last first middle) or direct order (first middle last). For all other indexes enter distinctive keywords.

  e.g., FIND PA JAMES. HENRY AND TI WINGS
        FIND SU ALCOHOL AND NOT FUEL
        FIND SE ENGLISH LITERARY STUDIES
        FIND TI MAGIC OR SU MAGIC

Modify completed search

AND/OR/AND NOT [index] [keyword(s)]. . .
  e.g., AND NOT TI MIDSUMMER DREAM
        AND SU ALCOHOL

Backup

BACKUP—to return to previous search result after a modification

Limit search result by date

AND DATE [year] / [year-year] / [-year] / [year-]
  e.g., AND DATE 1978
        AND DATE 1979–

Limit search result by campus location

AT [location]
  Campus locations:

UCB	UCSD	CLUSTER	MEDICAL
UCD	UCSF	HASTINGS	NORTH
UCI	UCSB	LAW	SOUTH
UCLA	UCSC	LBL	UC
UCR			

  e.g., AT UCSD
        AT MEDICAL

Truncation

Keywords may be right-truncated after 2 or more lette with the symbol #
  e.g., FIND SU BICYCL#

DISPLAY

DISPLAY [format] [record number(s)]
  Formats:
  REVIEW, BRIEF, LONG, MARC, field names
  e.g., DISPLAY ALL LONG
        DISPLAY AUTHOR TITLE 1–4, 6 8

BROWSE

BROWSE [index] [keyword(s)]
  e.g., BROWSE PA HEMINGWAY
        BROWSE SU ALCOHOL AND NOT FUEL
        BROWSE TI LIBR# AUTOMATI#

BROWSE [heading number(s)]
  e.g., BROWSE 10
        BROWSE 35–82

SELECT

SELECT [heading number(s)]
  e.g., SELECT 10 12
        SELECT 35–82

SHOW/SET/RESET

SHOW [setting]
  Settings:
  MODE   LIBRARIES   SEARCH
  FORMAT   SETTINGS   NEWS
  e.g., SHOW FORMAT
        SHOW SETTINGS

SET [setting] [desired setting]
  Settings that can be changed and their possible values:
  MODE (LOOKUP or COMMAND)
  FORMAT (REVIEW, BRIEF, LONG, MARC)
  LIBRARIES (see list under AT above)
  e.g., SET FORMAT LONG
        SET LIBRARY UCSD

RESET [setting]
  Settings that can be reset:
  MODE   LIBRARIES
  FORMAT
  e.g., RESET FORMAT

Number Searches

FIND [number index] [number]
  Number indexes:
  LCCN   ISSN
  ISBN
  e.g., FIND LCCN 79-300513

Quick guide to the command language of the University of California's online catalogue (MELVYL)

Free text searching, in some ways, is the most user-friendly of the various approaches because all that the user is required to do is to enter a search term. No menus are necessary, nor does the search term need to be preceded by a command such as FIND. A multiple field search is automatically generated.

For example, the user could type in the search term

TITANIC

and the following record might be retrieved and displayed:

KENNETT, FRANCES

THE GREATEST DISASTERS OF THE 20TH CENTURY

MARSHALL CAVENDISH, 1975

24 MAJOR CATASTROPHES INCLUDING THE SAN FRAN-CISCO EARTHQUAKE, THE TITANIC, THE HINDENBERG AND R101, HURRICANE FIFI AND ABERFAN

The search term appears only in the abstract but this makes no difference; relevant records will be retrieved no matter where the search term occurs.

Stringsearching, although extremely useful, can sometimes be slow (depending upon the system) and expensive, especially when searching through complex records in large files.

Qualifiers may be employed in some free text systems as limit factors to restrict the search. This can assist the user to define the requirement more clearly and may result in a faster response. For example, a search on

WHITING

would yield some items by or about persons of that name and also items on the subject as a type of fish. Inserting a qualifier, eg:

WHITING (AU)

would restrict the search to relevant *authors*.

Possible qualification parameters, which can be of general use, include language, type of publication and date of publication.

When a record is located, the computer will respond in different ways, dependent upon the system design, eg:

1 The retrieved record will be displayed immediately. If several records match the search term, these may be displayed together and 'scrolled' if screen capacity is exceeded. Alternatively they may be displayed and examined a screen at a time or a record at a time (see also page 96).

2 That portion of the catalogue sequence nearest to the search term will be displayed and the user may then select the record that he/she requires and perhaps request more detail relating to that particular item, eg:

```
FIND AUTHOR: DAVIS, D.

  1.    AUTHOR: DAVIS, C.
        TITLE: History of England          CLASS: 942

  2.    AUTHOR: DAVIS, D.
        TITLE: Gardening in colour         CLASS: 635

  3.    AUTHOR: BURROWS, F. ; DAVIS, D.
        TITLE: Aquarium fish               CLASS: 639.34

  4.    AUTHOR: DAVIS, D.V.
        TITLE: Modern domestic
               encyclopaedia               CLASS: 640.3

  5.    AUTHOR: JONES, M. ; DAVIS, D.W.
        TITLE: Pictorial home doctor       CLASS: 610

Choose from this list. Enter number here:
Then press 'SEND'
```

It may also be possible to browse forwards or backwards through the catalogue sequence, from this position, by entering, for example, 'F' or 'B' (see also page 100).

3 The computer will respond with

FOUND

or something similar (or NOT FOUND if no relevant items are retrieved) and the user must then enter a command such as

SHOW

or PRINT

to display the record on the screen.

When the number of records relevant to a particular search could be large, it may be necessary to provide an indication of the number of 'hits', eg:

23 RECORDS FOUND

The user may then need to refine the search. Alternatively, it may be possible to display a sample of the retrieved records, eg:

SHOW 3

to display the first three.

When a system is not directly related to a sequential file but merely checks for records or fields which contain the search term, then it is, of course, difficult to provide a 'browse' mechanism as indicated in (2) above.

Various levels of detail can sometimes be selected for display, eg title only, title, author and publisher, etc, and it may also be possible to select the order in which these elements are to appear.

For example, if ten records were retrieved after a search for the term CHESS as a keyword from title, then a command such as:

PRINT TITLE

might list the titles only of all ten items, so that the searcher could decide which titles were relevant before obtaining further details:

1 CHESS : THE END GAME
2 CHESS, EAST AND WEST, PAST AND PRESENT
3 CHESS PSYCHOLOGY
4 COMPUTER CHESS
5 ENCYCLOPAEDIA OF CHESS OPENINGS
6 HISTORY OF CHESS
7 KNOW THE GAME CHESS
8 PLAYING CHESS

9 RIGHT WAY TO PLAY CHESS
10 WORLD CHESS CHAMPIONSHIP

Some systems provide a full MARC display complete with tags, indicators, subfields, etc. Such a display is complex, can easily take up more than one screen, and is unsuitable for public consumption!

The various approaches are not mutually exclusive and dividing lines can sometimes be obscure. Some systems use a combination of the menu and command modes; others offer a choice between the two, and free text will still require a command language for the display of records once retrieved.

Whatever the approach, one or more of certain other features may also be provided for.

Truncation, for instance, enables the user to enter only part of a search term. This helps to compensate for the lack of a scan facility. For example, if the user does not know whether a required author's surname is spelled MILLIGAN or MILLIGEN, the truncation MILLIG can be searched for. Similarly, a search on the stem COMPUT will retrieve COMPUTER, COMPUTERS, COMPUTERIZATION, COMPUTING, etc. The truncation may be indicated by a symbol of some sort, eg:

        COMPUT:
or   COMPUT#

or it may be implicit.

It is possible to use truncation on classification numbers, eg:

        72   All works on architecture
        726   All works on buildings for religious purposes
        726.6   All works on cathedrals

Some systems allow front truncation as well as back truncation. For example, if the user is not sure whether an author is spelled ELIOTT or ELLIOTT, then a search on

        #LIOTT

would yield items indexed under either spelling.

'Wild card' characters can cater for searches which involve

variant spellings, plurals, etc. ORGANI#ATION will search for ORGANISATION or ORGANIZATION; M#N will search for MAN and MEN.

It is often possible to link search terms by means of the logical operators 'AND', 'OR' and 'NOT'.

A search on

GLASS AND CRYSTAL

would yield all items indexed under *both* these terms.

A search on

GLASS OR CRYSTAL

would yield all items indexed under *either* of the two terms.

A search on

GLASS NOT CRYSTAL

would yield all items indexed under GLASS but *not* those indexed under CRYSTAL.

Such logic may be used to help refine searches. For example, a search on

EDUCATION

might yield

SET 1: 500 RECORDS FOUND

A search on

COMPUTERS

might yield

SET 2: 700 RECORDS FOUND

and finally, a search on

LIBRARIANSHIP

might yield

SET 3: 200 RECORDS FOUND

The three searches could then be linked, eg:

SET 1 AND SET 2 AND SET 3

or   1 AND 2 AND 3

and the resultant yield, in terms of the number of items found, will obviously be considerably reduced to more manageable proportions.

Terms may also be linked by relational operators such as 'greater than', 'less than', or 'equal to', usually symbolized by $>$, $<$, or $=$ respectively. For example:

FIND SUBJECT MOON AND DATE $>$ 1984

would yield all items on the subject of the moon with a date later than 1984.

Proximity, or 'position' operators are sometimes employed in free text searching to enable the searcher to specify the position of search terms relative to one another. For example:

FIND WALL W2 DEATH

would retrieve 'Wall of death' (W2 meaning within two words); This can be helpful, especially if such a phrase appears, for example, in an abstract and the word 'of' is included on a stoplist and not indexed.

'Approximation' searching allows for spelling errors in user input.

In some systems, it may be possible to examine the thesaurus of indexing terms online. For example, the thesaurus entry shown on page 00 might be displayed on the screen thus:

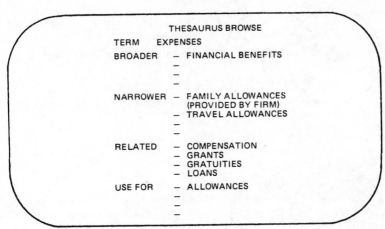

An unusual feature recently introduced in the National Library of Medicine's (US) CITE public access catalogue is 'weighted' or 'ranked' searching. Subject queries are entered in plain English, eg

: community health services for the elderly and the handicapped[1]

and CITE retrieves and displays related textwords, subject headings and subheadings:

RANK TERM
1 COMMUNITY HEALTH SERVICES (medical subject heading)
2 COMMUNITY MENTAL HEALTH SERVICES (medical subject heading)
3 ELDERLY (text word)
4 IN OLD AGE (subheading)
5 HANDICAPPED (text word)
. . .
11 SERVICES (text word)
12 CENTRAL SUPPLY, HOSPITAL (medical subject heading)
. . .
14 HEALTH (text word)
etc

The user then selects from this list the numbers of those

1 CITE/NLM : natural language searching in an online catalog / Tamas E. Doszkocs *Information technology and libraries* 2 (4) December 1983 364-380

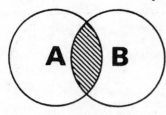

Logical *product* — the 'and' search
Symbolized as A.B, A × B or (A) (B)
All documents dealing with 'mathematics' and 'teaching'

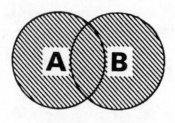

Logical *sum* — the 'not' search
Symbolized as A + B
All documents on 'mathematics' *or* 'teaching'

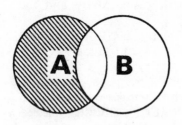

Logical *difference* — the 'not' search
Symbolized as A − B
All documents on 'mathematics' but *not* 'the teaching of mathematics'

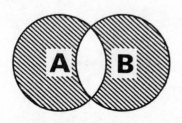

Exclusive 'or' search
Symbolized as
(A + B) − (A × B)
All documents on 'mathematics' *or* 'teaching' but *not* 'the teaching of mathematics'

Boolean logic searching. Circle A represents all of the documents present in a database dealing with the subject 'mathematics' and circle B all of the documents dealing with the subject 'teaching'

search terms most relevant to the search, ranked in their order of importance, or types in ALL if every term is required. The search uses a combinatorial 'best match' technique, rather than Boolean logic.[1]

As can be seen, the above system makes use of inbuilt authority control. Terms related to the search terms entered by the user are indicated. It is possible, with inbuilt online authority control, to switch from the term entered automatically so that, for example, whether the user enters MARIHUANA or CANNABIS relevant records will still be retrieved (see page 61). However, switching from the term as entered without informing the user may cause confusion in certain areas, eg personal names. Retrieved records, when displayed, may not contain the original search term.

FIND AUTHOR AMIS, KINGSLEY

might produce the result:

1 AMIS, KINGSLEY LUCKY JIM. 1954
2 MARKHAM, ROBERT COLONEL SUN. 1968

It could be advantageous to provide the user with some indication of what is happening, eg

1 AMIS, KINGSLEY LUCKY JIM. 1954
The name that you entered: AMIS, KINGSLEY
is also entered in this catalogue under: MARKHAM, ROBERT
Do you wish to continue the search? YES/NO?

However, it is appreciated that this would make the system more complex.

Searching may not be via an actual name or term but through a search code made up of characters that appear in the terms required (derived search keys). A 4,3,1 author code, for example, would consist of the first four letters of the author's surname, the first three letters of the first forename and the initial of the second forename, if any, eg:

MOOR,PET,G = MOORE, PETER G

---

1 *NLM's online public access catalog.* — National Library of Medicine. Factsheet, September 1983

Characters may be extracted from more than one field; a code for author and title could consist of the first four letters of the author's surname, the first word of the title (excluding articles) and the first letters of the next two title words, if any, eg:

WELLWAROT = WELLS WAR OF THE WORLDS

Such search patterns may, however, be restricted to staff use as it could well be difficult to train users to construct the necessary codes.

In an online system, it is not unusual for a user to find him or herself in a position of not knowing what to do next. It is therefore useful to have a 'help' feature to cater for this situation. The user can type in

HELP

at any time and guidance will be given. (See also page 114.)

With the various facilities as detailed above, it is clear that online searching can be very flexible. It is easy for the computer to handle searches which would be extremely difficult, if not impossible, in a manual system, eg

'What tape/slide presentations on the computer, published later than 1983, are available which are suitable for eleven year olds?'

or 'What works on Liverpool have been published in Liverpool?'

The search methods so far described involve the use of a keyboard and the 'typing' of relevant commands and search terms. It is also possible to have a keyboard-free terminal where input is via a touch-sensitive screen. Beneath the surface of the screen are heat-sensitive pads and users touch words on the screen to indicate what they require. This overcomes user problems such as lack of keyboarding skills and spelling difficulties.

The first user instruction for instance, might be:

1 Touch START OVER to begin search

and the second:

2 Touch the name of the file you wish to search:

    TITLE
    AUTHOR
    SUBJECT

After the user has touched the required file name, the screen displays a broad alphabetic selection. The user narrows this down by touching the entry that comes alphabetically or numerically before the one for which he/she is searching. This procedure is repeated until the desired item appears.

Suppose that, after the file name TITLE has been touched, the following selection appears:

    AIRCRAFT OF WORLD WAR II
    CASTLES OF WALES
    DISCOVER AMERICA
    GIRLS' GYMNASTICS
    MODERN DOMESTIC ENCYCLOPAEDIA
    POPULAR PET KEEPING
    RA EXPEDITIONS
    THEY FEARED NO EVIL
    USING COMPUTERS
    YACHTMASTER'S GUIDE

If the user were searching for the title SHAPING UP TO FASHION, then, according to the instructions, the title RA EXPEDITIONS would be touched and this would cause a further display:

    RA EXPEDITIONS
    RELIGIONS OF THE WORLD
    ROAD SAFETY
    ROMAN LIFE
    RUG MAKING
    SAILING IS FUN
    SHRUBS FOR THE GARDEN
    SOUTH-AMERICAN INDIANS
    STATISTICS IN ACTION
    TANKS IN MODERN WARFARE

SAILING IS FUN is now the title which comes before the one that is required and, when this is touched, the

Public Access Catalog Instructions

1 Touch *START OVER* to begin or end your search.

2 Touch the name of the file you wish to search: TITLE, AUTHOR, SUBJECT

A
B
C
D
E
F
G
H
I
J
K
L
M
N
O
P
Q
R
S
T
U
V
W
X
Y
Z

3 Touch the entry which comes alphabetically or numerically before the one for which you are searching. *Numbers file before letters.*

4 Repeat Step 3 until you see *BROWSE-REVERSE* and *BROWSE-FORWARD* at the bottom of the screen.

5 The entry you are looking for should now be listed on the screen. If not, the library does not have it, *OR* it is listed under another spelling or heading.

6 Now touch the term you selected to get a list of materials the library owns.

7 If there is more than one entry, continue to touch *SCROLL UP* to see them one by one.

8 When you see a title you want, *touch it* to get complete information, including whether copies may be on the shelf or checked out. (You must wait several seconds for this information.)

9 The screen now shows you the information the card catalog gave you. In addition you will see:

  (1) EVK 3 1192 00000 7528 (2) 6/15/81 (3)
     ENK 3 1192 00000 7215 (2) ON SHELF (4)

1. Code for main library or branch where item is located (code explained on reverse side of sheet).

2. Item number for each copy owned.

3. Indicates that this copy is checked out and is due back on the date shown.

4. Indicates this copy may be on the shelf. Write down the call number for locating it. Call number is in the upper left hand corner of screen.

10 If the call number says *ONORD* (on order) or *REC'D* (received), the material has been ordered or has been received for the Library's collection.

11 Touch *PAGE NEXT* to see if there is more information about this item. (Repeated beeps mean all information is on the first screen.)

12 Touch *START OVER* to end your search or to begin another. If you need assistance. ask a librarian or touch *HELP*.

PAC instructions as used by Iowa City Public Library (US)

following might be the result:

    SAILING IS FUN
    SAFETY IN SMALL CRAFT
    SATELLITES AND COMMUNICATION
    SCIENCE MAKES SENSE
    SCOTTISH SPLENDOUR
    SEA FISHING
    SELF-DEFENCE THE EXPERT'S WAY
    SEX AND THE SINGLE GIRL

SHAPING UP TO FASHION
SHIPS OF THE ST LAWRENCE

This selection includes the required title and a further touch will obtain further details of the item.

The first library to provide this type of access to public catalogues was the Chicago suburb of Evanston and other libraries in the United States quickly followed suit. The system is referred to by the acronym PAC (Public Access Catalog). (The acronym OPAC is usually used to refer to any Online Public Access Catalogue.)

It is obviously less 'direct' and slower to select progressively from lists of entries rather than type in a search term and receive an immediate response. Users also have to remember the A—Z order which is, apparently, a more serious drawback than it sounds for instructions may now include a display of the alphabet. Nevertheless this is an innovative and extremely interesting development.

A CLSI (CL Systems Inc.) keyboard-free touch terminal in operation

This chapter has described a pot-pourri of possibilities for searching computer produced catalogues. It is not claimed to be exhaustive for a vast number of systems proliferate, varying from large networks using co-operative mainframe facilities to the small one-person library with an in-house microcomputer. This review, however, should have provided a good indication of the wide range of methodologies.

A final point to be made is that, at the present time, not all public online catalogues have a subject access facility yet one of the major findings of the CLR sponsored survey referred to on page 96 was that there is a need for such a feature. Simonds maintains that the problem lies with the MARC database itself as the LC MARC record does not provide adequate subject access. 'The weaknesses of Library of Congress subject cataloging are well known . . . and the only hope for adequate subject access is through fundamental changes in the national standard.'[1] UK MARC includes PRECIS (PREserved Context Index System) entries which can be used for online retrieval. PRECIS (see also page 109) is a specially developed computer produced pre-coordinate indexing method. According to Kilgour, pre-coordinate indexing is better than post-coordinate, in which the terms are coordinated by the searcher, for online access because the latter puts a heavy burden on both the user and the computer.[2]

The Library of Congress made a study of PRECIS some years ago and concluded that it liked it as a mode of accessing material. Unfortunately, adopting it as well as continuing the assignment of Library of Congress subject headings — a sine qua non, according to the views of the American librarian community — would have meant an increase in operating costs of approximately $1,000,000 per annum.

1 Database limitations & online catalogs / Michael J. Simonds *Library journal* 109 (3) February 15 1984
2 The online catalog revolution / Frederick G. Kilgour *op. cit.*

Chapter Eight

Management aspects

The benefits of a computerized cataloguing system, as out-lined in Chapter 1, are indisputable but a decision to automate or not to automate the catalogue will depend upon a great many additional factors, including:

Size and type of library
Staffing levels
Financial support
Computer availability

Computerizing the catalogue might be difficult, for example, in a small one-person library with very restricted financial provision and no access to any sort of computer. It is appreciated that some small libraries, unfortunately, cannot afford even an adequate bookstock, let alone consider automation. On the other hand, a large academic library with considerable resources and, in all probability, access to a mainframe might find it difficult to *resist* automation.

It is not unknown, however, in the case of the small library, for things to change overnight and if, for instance, a chance were suddenly offered to purchase a microcomputer system, as might happen in a school or college library, then the possi-bility of automation would have to be reviewed.

This is not, of course, to imply that the larger library will *always* find it easy to automate. A number of sizeable library systems, such as the public libraries of the cities of Liverpool and Manchester, continue to have to manage with manual catalogues.

Systems analysis (see also Glossary)
The term 'systems analysis' is commonly used to cover all aspects which are involved in ensuring that a computerized

system works effectively and with the maximum possible efficiency. Systems analysis is not solely concerned with computers but is currently associated more with those situations which might benefit from the use of a computer than with any others.

The more specific meaning of the term relates to the examination of an existing method of operation in order to ascertain whether computerization might lead to an improvement. In other words, before adopting an automated system, it is necessary to define objectives and then undertake a *feasibility study*.

The feasibility study will examine the various ways that the defined objectives might be achieved and it will look at the costs that might be incurred in relation to the benefit accrued (cost-benefit analysis). It will also investigate cost effectiveness in terms of manpower. If, for instance, a feasibility study concluded, as it did in one Australian library, that the cost of continuing with a manual cataloguing system would be $5,000 more, over a five year period, than a computer MARC-based system and would take some 17,500 extra man hours over the same period,[1] then the obvious recommendation would be an automated system.

Options
When a library does plan to automate its catalogue, there are a number of options that it might choose from:
1 To 'go-it-alone' and develop an independent in-house system
2 To have a complete 'turnkey' package installed by a commercial supplier
3 To make use of a centralized cataloguing service such as MARC
4 To join a co-operative network
5 To choose a viable combination of the above, eg 2 and 3, or 3 and 4.

Going it alone
The 'go-it-alone' system can vary from a single microcomputer configuration to the sophisticated set-up with mainframe

1 Feasibility study for an automated cataloguing system / Peter James and Pam Ray *LASIE* 9 (4) January/February 1979 34-41

support. Software will be written in-house or consist of an appropriate 'off-the-shelf' package. The development of suitable software can be a tedious, time-consuming and costly business and many libraries will therefore prefer to purchase a ready made solution. However, there is sometimes a friendly and willing computer services department (in a college for instance) which may offer assistance.

One example of a college library which acquired a microcomputer and wrote programs in-house is the West Suffolk College of Further Education (UK) (the library borrowed a 32K Pet from the management department and ran a demonstration of an issue system on it in order to persuade the college authorities to spend the necessary money). The programs were written by a part-time member of the library staff who was also a maths graduate. Within a month of the arrival of a 48K Apple II, the first program was operational. This would sort and list the periodical holdings of the library into alphabetical or classified order, search for a particular title or class number, and add or delete titles.[1]

The programs used by Sefton Libraries (see also page 25) were developed for the library service by the local authority's Treasurer's Department. Plessey were also involved, however, as the firm's automated circulation control system was being installed at the same time.

If in-house development is chosen, care should be taken to ensure that on-going back-up and maintenance are available and that enhancement will be possible as and when necessary. It is not unknown for an in-house system to grind to a halt as it grew and developed due to the lack of such facilities. Of course, at the time when libraries such as West Suffolk College were developing their own software, there were very few packaged programs designed specifically for libraries. The situation is now very different. Indeed, West Suffolk College currently makes use of packages obtained from outside the institution.

The prime example of an in-house development is probably the University of California's MELVYL system, which is one of the most sophisticated and advanced public online cataloguing systems in existence.

1 Advent of micros offer many possibilities / Robin Shreeve *Educational computing* 2 (6) June 1981 37-38

Sources additional to software developed in-house are:

1 The computer manufacturers themselves

IBM, for example, have available a package called STAIRS for use on their machines. The acronym stands for STorage And Information Retrieval System. This is a powerful, free text retrieval system which enables stringsearching from any part of a record. STAIRS is used in the Clwyd Library Service (UK) to manage a database which contains bibliographic records of items in the Community Information Collection and records of societies and organizations in Clwyd.

Also available from IBM is DOBIS/LEUVEN, an on-line cataloguing system which was originally developed jointly by IBM and the University of Dortmund library. This package is used by a number of libraries including the National Library of Canada, Leuven University Library (Belgium) and University College Cork (Ireland). The cost of this software is $50,000.

2 Other commercial suppliers (software houses or private organizations)

One could not begin to list all of these. Some packages have been developed over a period of many years and have wide information retrieval applications, cataloguing being just one of the many functions that can be performed. One example of a package which has become widely recognized as a major tool in information handling is ASSASSIN (Agricultural System for Storage And Subsequent Selection of InformatioN), which is written in a version of COBOL, and which will run on IBM, ICL and DEC machines. Originally used internally at ICI Agricultural Division (UK) during the 1960s, it was publicly released in 1972. It has since been further enhanced, eg current awareness (1974/5), interactive searching (1978), and has been sold to a considerable number of organizations. ASSASSIN includes standard features for handling large scale databases but the latest version was designed with an office environment in mind. It attempts to ensure that it is easy for users to enter information, find it again, annotate information and deliver documents to other users (electronic mail).

Another example of a package which is wide ranging but which could be applied to cataloguing type operations is CAIRS (Computer Assisted Information Retrieval System), which was developed at the Food Research Association (UK), initially as an in-house system to replace the card files and printed keyword indexes. Smith Kline & French Laboratories is one institution making use of this package and the intention is to automatically index all words in document titles (apart from those on a stoplist) and constituent elements of Universal Decimal Classification numbers.

Packages such as ASSASSIN and CAIRS are intended for mainframes or minicomputers and they can cost anything from £5,000 to £30,000 or even more depending upon content. Lower down the scale are the cheaper packages for the microcomputer. CAIRS is, in fact, also available as MicroCAIRS (from RTZ Computer Services of Bristol (UK), and costing from £1,400 to £5,000 for various versions). MicroCAIRS will run on machines such as the IBM Personal Computer and the ACT Sirius. Suitable hardware to support the system costs approximately £6,000 upwards. The package offers high speed Boolean searches on over 10,000 records with total user definition of database record structure and an optional thesaurus facility. It is upwards compatible and portable to larger multi-user minicomputers.

A recent report on library software for microcomputers, which does not pretend to be exhaustive and which excludes general purpose software (which could well be suitable for library needs) lists over 50 packages designed to produce catalogues or information retrieval systems.[1]

One further example of a microcomputer package from a commercial supplier which is suitable for cataloguing is LIBRARIAN. This is available from Eurotec Consultants Ltd, Colchester (UK). A standard off-the-shelf version costs £450 and fully tailored systems usually fall into the range £1,250–£1,450. LIBRARIAN is written in a version of PASCAL which runs on most 8 and 16 bit microcomputers which utilize CP/M-80

---

1 *Library software for microcomputers* / compiled by Hilary Gates. — Oxford : Cairns Library, John Radcliffe Hospital, 1984. — (British Library R&D report No. 5798)

or CP/M-86 operating systems.[1] A version of LIBRARIAN is in use at the University of Buckingham Library based on a Comart Communicator with a 20 megabyte hard disc which it is estimated will accommodate some 40,000 catalogue entries, 60,000 related subject index entries and a similar quantity of classification numbers. An important feature of LIBRARIAN is that the size of the database that it can handle is not constrained by the operating system. As the library's catalogue grows, therefore, all that will be required is to increase the disc capacity.[2,3] (See also pages 45 and 113.)

3 Institutions using compatible equipment for similar operations

There are obvious advantages in being able to obtain tried and tested software from another institution of comparable size and with broadly the same general objectives. In 1973/4, for example, Derbyshire Libraries (UK) acquired the programs used by the Cheshire Library Service:

'The only ready-made system that provided what the Working Party proposed as requisite for Derbyshire was the computerised book ordering and cataloguing system (not using MARC but MARC compatible) introduced by Cheshire Library Service in 1972. The Cheshire computer was compatible with that of Derbyshire hence the time consuming and costly programming and testing could be reduced. Also the Cheshire system was similar in scale (ie in stock and number of libraries) to the proposed new Derbyshire Library Service.'[4]

Subsequently, Derbyshire, in co-operation with other bodies, developed and enhanced the system and:

'interestingly the wheel turned full circle in 1980

---

1 *Librarian − cataloguing and enquiry* / Eurotec Consultants. Publicity leaflet June 1984
2 Selecting software for a micro-based library catalogue / John E. Pemberton *The law librarian* (14) December 1983 35-38
3 Cataloguing on a micro with Librarian / John E. Pemberton *op. cit.*
4 What price independence / Peter Gratton *Catalogue & index* (62) Autumn 1981 1-4

for Cheshire acquired the system pioneered by Derbyshire.'[1]

In the United States, a number of locally developed systems are now being offered for sale to other libraries. One example is the Virginia Tech Library System (VTLS) which uses a Hewlett Packard minicomputer. However, the library 'soon discovered that selling, installing, supporting and maintaining automated systems in a number of libraries placed demands on the VTLS staff and resources for which they were ill prepared.'[2] In 1984 an agreement was reached for Hewlett Packard to market while VTLS staff will continue to maintain the system. A further example is the Northwestern University's NOTIS (NOrthwestern Total library Information System) which can run on an IBM mainframe or minicomputer.

The computer bureau
One possibility that might be considered within the context of 'going-it-alone' is the processing of a library's data by a commercial bureau. The bureau will normally permit the use of its computer for any task for which the customer is willing to pay. The library need not then concern itself with the provision of hardware nor worry too much about technological advances and equipment updates. The bureau, if it wishes to remain competitive, will change its equipment as necessary. Usually, the provision of software will also be the responsibility of the bureau.

Currently, the probability is that such a service will operate in batch, offline mode, the library supplying the bureau with the necessary data and the bureau then producing a catalogue on paper or fiche. However, an online service is also possible and the library will then have to acquire terminals to access the system.

In general terms, the nearer the library is to the bureau the better, for this will reduce such overheads as transport or line communication costs, and library and bureau staff will be able to meet more easily to discuss problems. Turn around

1 *ibid.*
2 Competition & change : the 1983 automated library system marketplace / Joseph R. Matthews *Library journal* 109 (8) May 1 1984 853-860

times are obviously of importance in a batch system and, if online access is provided, the number of hours that access is permitted becomes a vital factor.

When contemplating the use of a bureau, a service that is well established should be sought and attempts made to ensure that there are safeguards should the firm run into problems. For example, how easy is it to transfer to another system?

The above detail relates to the use of a bureau for all computer based operations, the library merely supplying eye-readable data. There is, of course, the alternative of a library supplying the bureau with machine-readable data from which an appropriate catalogue form, eg microfiche, can be produced. However, in this case, some of the problems of hardware and software acquisition remain with the library.

Acquiring a package

When considering the acquisition of a package, it is useful, if not essential, for the prospective purchaser to be able to assess its potential by actually seeing it in operation. A demonstration should be requested together with a list of the names of other users so that they may be approached for their views and opinions. More than one possibility should be examined in order to obtain some idea of operational and performance variations.

When deciding which package is right for a particular institution's cataloguing needs, it is also helpful to follow a systematic procedure and to establish criteria by which the suitability of the package may be judged.

If computer equipment is already available to the institution, then the first questions that should be asked are:

1 Can the package be used on this equipment? What operating system does the package use? Is this compatible with the available hardware?

2 Is the available hardware capacious enough in terms of immediate access and secondary storage?

After this, or if the package is to be chosen first and appropriate hardware obtained later, some detail relating to relevant criteria such as the following should be prepared so that the package can be measured against system requirement:

1 The record format to be used, including the number of fields, the maximum number of characters per field and the number of fields per record.

2 The maximum number of records that the system will need to cater for.

3 The type of manipulations that will be required, eg adding, deleting, amending, searching (specifying the *kind* of searching required, eg stringsearching), sorting, etc.

If the package is to be operated by the library user as well as library staff, confirmation should be sought that the user can be prevented from corrupting the database. It is also important to try and discover what performance will be like with the amount of data that the institution intends to store (search times, for instance, can increase alarmingly as files grow in size). If it is intended to produce hard copy output such as booklists, facilities for 'report' generation should be examined.

The above information gives some indication of the features that should be monitored when assessing a package. It is by no means exhaustive, however, there are further questions that could be pertinent; some examples follow:

1 Entering the data

How easy is this?

How easy is it to make amendments, for example to go back to amend a mistake in an earlier field?

2 Displaying the data

Can fields be placed anywhere on the vdu screen, ie can the record be rearranged?

Do all fields have to be displayed or can some be hidden?

Can the field names be suppressed?

3 Number of files

Can multiple files be handled and can they be inter-related?

Where the larger, more sophisticated online public access catalogues are concerned, Hildreth[1] identifies four functional areas which may be used to classify command capability and thus facilitate comparisons between systems. These areas are:
1 Operational control; 2 Searching (including Access points);
3 Output control; 4 User assistance. (1) includes not only logon and logoff procedures but the availability/non-avail-

1 *Online public access catalogs : the user interface* / Charles R. Hildreth *op. cit.*

ability of facilities such as editing (erasure and modification
of input), stacking (entry of multiple commands at the one
time), the 'saving' of search statements, and the interruption
of online output. (2) includes possible search features such as
free text, Boolean logic, truncation, etc. Access points could
include author, title, author/title combined, subject, control
number, ISBN, or other search terms. Where (3) is concerned,
examples of possible features are choice of output format,
browsing, sorting, and hard copy printouts. (4) relates to the
amount of help that can be obtained by the user, eg the
listing of commands for review, the examination of index or
thesaurus terms, the display of a search history, the explanation of system messages, or the use of 'tutorials' (instructional lessons provided by the system).

Requirements should be discussed with the supplier and
an attempt made to ascertain how well the package meets
them. Even the simplest of questions may be important.

If the supplier is a dealer, then ensure that this is a reputable
and dependable dealer who can provide help with installation,
maintenance and support. Use a dealer that has been personally recommended or look for one which displays a helpful
and professional attitude. If the firm is a member of an
appropriate association, eg the Computer Retailers Association
in the UK, then this is a helpful indicator of competence.

In general, superfluous embellishments should be ignored;
the emphasis should be on finding a package that will do the
job efficiently and in a user-friendly manner. It should be
remembered that well-written and easy to follow documentation is an essential requisite.

Lists of software are issued by computer manufacturers,
retailers and software houses. The *Software publishers'
catalogs annual* (Meckler Publishing, $97.50) is a microfiche
version of many of these catalogues. A number of general
software directories are available, eg: *Software catalog*
(formerly *International software directory*) in two volumes,
one covering microcomputers and the other minis. This can
be obtained in hard copy from ISD at $69 per issue but it is
also available online as *International software directory*[1]
through Dialog. Other directories are also available online.
Patrick Dewey has provided a recent checklist of directories:
Searching for software : a checklist of microcomputer software
directories *Library journal* 109 (5) March 15 1984 544-546.

1 Now entitled: *.Menu — international software database*

It is possible, of course, to commission a software house to develop a package specifically tailored to a particular library's needs.

Before leaving the subject of packages, it should be noted that software need not necessarily provide for a complete cataloguing system. A variety of programs are available which can perform various of the constituent cataloguing functions. If, for instance, a library wishes to retain a manual card catalogue but wants some assistance in the production of the cards, there is a great deal of appropriate software available. Examples are CARDPREP from the Library Software Company, Pleasant Hill, CA (US), at $199 (requires Apple II or TRS-80); and CARD from Capital Systems Group, Kensington, MD 20895 (US) at $300, which requires a CP/M operating system and which prints catalogue cards according to AACR2.

If a keyword index is required, some of the packages already noted, eg ASSASSIN, CAIRS and MicroCAIRS, include suites of programs for this purpose. Another example of a suitable package is MICROPSI. This is a suite of programs for the production of indexes by microcomputer. Two types of index may be produced, KWAC (Key Word and Context) and NEPHIS (NEsted PHase Indexing System), first developed in Canada by T C Craven. MICROPSI is available from the College of Librarianship Wales; it requires a CP/M operating system.

Examples of other cataloguing related functions for which software can be obtained are bibliography production and book indexing. BIBLIOGRAPHY COMPILER is a cheap, cassette based program which is available from Libraries and Learning Inc, New York, at $20 (runs on Apple, Commodore Pet or TRS-80). PERSONAL BIBLIOGRAPHIC SYSTEM is a more sophisticated program for compiling and maintaining bibliographies. This is available from Personal Bibliographic Software, Ann Arbor, MI (US) at $250 and it integrates with DATA TRANSFER SYSTEM from the same company at $200. The latter can be used to download and reformat records from online catalogues such as OCLC and RLIN (see pages 169–70) to form a bibliography. These programs will run on a number of computers including Apple, IBM Personal and Victor 9000. A package which indexes books and reports, BOOKDEX, is available from

1 Ability to perform specified tasks
2 Ease of operation
3 Vendor stability
4 Other users' reports
5 Speed of operation
6 Ease of configuration to user's particular requirements
7 Support from supplier
8 Quality of documentation

Checklist of the eight most important criteria for evaluating software as identified and ranked in order of importance by Look (Evaluating software for microcomputers / Hugh Evison Look The electronic library *2 (1) January 1984 53-60). Other criteria listed by Look are given below, although these are not ranked, as priorities will vary from user to user:*

    i Adaptability, eg to various machines
   ii Expansion potential as library or information service grows
  iii Size limitations, in file or record, imposed by hardware or software
  iv Security, ie facilities for access via passwords
   v Multi-user potential
  vi Environment limitations, ie machine or operating system restrictions
vii Trial period before final contract
  ix Published reviews

Capital Systems Group, Kensington, MD (US) at $450. NEWSDEX, from the same firm, also at $450, prepares and cumulates newspaper indexes. VIEWIndex (£14.95 from Acornsoft, C/o Vector Marketing, Wellingborough, Northants, UK) is an automatic index generator on disc for use with VIEW (£59.80), a word processing system which is programmed onto a 16K plug-in ROM chip for the BBC microcomputer.

At the extreme lower end of the scale, this author recently came across a Dewey Decimal Classification subject index

F

Extracts from a printed book index produced by microcomputer, the typesetting being done automatically from disc. The program used here is Microindex which currently runs on an Apple II. Farestead Associates (24 Astley Road, Hemel Hempstead, UK) are using the program to do indexing work, especially for journals needing cumulative indexes. However, they were planning to have a version available for sale by the end of 1984.

which had been created on cassette tape (complete with sound effects!) by a group of sixth form students for use with a BBC microcomputer. This was on sale for a few pounds (from Aztec Software, Sheffield, UK). Although not very detailed, this could have its uses in a small school library.

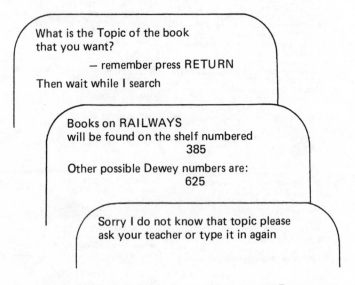

What is the Topic of the book
that you want?
          — remember press RETURN
Then wait while I search

Books on RAILWAYS
will be found on the shelf numbered
                385
Other possible Dewey numbers are:
                625

Sorry I do not know that topic please
ask your teacher or type it in again

Sample screens from the Aztec Dewey Computer Program

Turnkey systems

An alternative to the purchase of separate hardware and software, is the acquisition of a 'turnkey' (as easy as turning a key in a lock — no prior knowledge necessary) system. This comprises both hardware and software which can be quickly installed without the need to consider relative compatibility. One of the world leaders in the provision of this type of system is Geac Computers International. Geac provides a total package, including prior consultation to discover the specific needs of the institution, the design of a system to meet these requirements, and the installation, commissioning and maintenance of this system. Geac's own hardware forms the basic configuration.

   Geac can provide a simple to use public online catalogue system which claims to provide fast and sophisticated bibliographic information accessed by author, title, class or any control number. In addition, keyword and boolean searching can be implemented. Geac also offers authority control and compatibility with MARC.

Geac is Canadian based with general computer interests. The company installed an online library system in two Canadian universities (Waterloo and Guelph) in the late 1970s. Installations at other libraries followed and library based activities were extended to Europe. The first Geac library system in the UK was inaugurated at the University of Hull in 1980. The basic system provided for interactive circulation control backed up by an online bibliographic database which was able to perform as a catalogue. The London Borough of Hillingdon recently became the first public library in the UK to contract to take all of the software currently available from Geac. Online catalogues became available to the public in September, 1983.

In late 1983, a series of co-operative efforts were announced between Geac and the Faxon Company that would link Geac's integrated systems with Faxon's LINX network for online searching of LINX databases, tape exchange and communications.[1]

Whilst the Geac system is built around the company's own hardware, other suppliers of turnkey systems see versatility as being of prime importance. Oriel Computer Services, from Chipping Norton, Oxon (UK), have an online cataloguing system which is available for a wide range of computing systems, including Sirius 1, Victor 9000 and IBM Personal. The first of these Oriel systems, based on a Sirius, was delivered to Her Majesty's Stationery Office for the cataloguing of HMSO publications and the production of Daily List catalogues in 1982.[2]

In North America, the market leader of turnkey online packages, in terms of numbers sold, is CLSI (CL Systems Inc — see also page 129) followed by Geac and Dataphase.[3] These systems are minicomputer based and usually they are linked to a circulation control system. North America is the clear leader in terms of the number of public online catalogues. 'There are at least 37 different systems and possibly as many

1 *Information technology and libraries* 2 (4) December 1983 450
2 *Oriel news* (3) February 1983 3
3 Competition & change : the 1983 automated library system marketplace / Joseph R. Matthews *op. cit.*

as 200 libraries with an operational online catalogue'.[1] Systems have also been installed outside the US and Canada; the CLSI LIBS-100, for example, is used at the Royal Melbourne Institute of Technology (Australia).

Another turnkey package which has crossed national boundaries is URICA. This originated in South Africa where it was developed by Unicom as a cataloguing system using relational database techniques. In Australia, it is known as AWA URICA after the firm that adapted it to handle the Australian MARC (AUSMARC) and that also markets it. It is available in the UK under licence through Microdata. URICA is used, for example, in Australia, at the Ryde Munici-

CATALOGUING REQUIREMENTS

The requirements of a modern machine assisted cataloguing system are:

● Inter-active working at least on the cataloguing side, for review of bought-in records and for local cataloguing.

● Easy to use screen formats as close as possible to 'traditional' catalogue displays.

● The removal of machine related codings from the screen as much as possible.

● Machine assisted cataloguing decision making.

● Links with the Ordering, Circulation and Periodicals control modules.

● Efficient establishment of processing links with files external to the library, for record acquisition or bibliographical information.

● Easy to use access facilities on line, including both 'browsing' sequences and logical connectives processing.

● The ability to provide hard copy lists and catalogues, ranging from simple results of searching to full scale complete catalogues, microform, laser printed, etc.

Requirements of a computerized cataloguing system as seen by Oriel Computer Services

---

1 Online public access to library files in North America / Alan Seal *Vine* (53) April 1984 33-37

pal Library and the Library Board of Western Australia in integrated library systems.[1]

Centralized cataloguing services

Centralized cataloguing relates to a situation where one central agency assumes responsibility for the production of cataloguing data which is then made available to any library that may require it. Such an agency and the libraries which it serves may, of course, be part of a single library system but the central provider could also be an external agency which makes cataloguing information available for payment. The concept of centralized cataloguing, in the latter sense, is not new. The Library of Congress provides an outstanding example of such a service. Since 1901 it has made available printed cards containing its cataloguing data. Today, the LC Cataloging Distribution Service (CDS) produces cards on-demand from machine-readable records (the CARDS system) and also utilizes an optical-disc-based storage, preservation and printing system that allows CDS to access and reproduce on demand more than 5.5 million catalogue cards in hundreds of different languages that are not in machine-readable form (the DEMAND system). The two systems mean the prompt fulfilment of libraries' orders for catalogue cards without the necessity of maintaining a large inventory of stock. In the UK, the British National Bibliography introduced a card service in 1956. The BNB cards are now produced using a laser printer which gives the cards an enhanced appearance when compared with cards produced by other computer printers. For automated cataloguing, however, it is not cards that are required but the actual machine-readable data itself. As previously noted, both the Library of Congress and the British Library make such data available from the MARC bases in punched card or magnetic tape format.

The use of such a service may simply mean subscribing to buy individual records from the MARC bases for processing on the individual library's own computer (a selective record service). Selected records can be identified by control number (eg ISBN (International Standard Book Number), BNB (British National Bibliography) number, or LC (Library of

1 AWA-URICA library systems / Pat Manson *Vine* (53) April 1984 13-28

Congress) number). Records purchased in this way will be full MARC records. Alternatively, records could be selected online, as with the BLAISE (British Library Automated Information SErvice) system, and edited to conform to the requirements of the individual library. This could include deletion or amendment of fields and the addition of local data. With this BLAISE package it is also possible to create new records for items not contained in the central database (EMMA — Extra MARC material).

The complete MARC bases can be mounted on a library's computer if so desired and these are then kept up to date by a weekly tape of current records.

At the other end of the scale, those libraries who wish it can opt for a complete cataloguing service such as that offered by the British Library's LOCAS (LOcal CAtaloguing Service). LOCAS covers everything from data preparation to cataloguing production for libraries wanting to take full advantage of a centralized system, although if the specific library has some local facilities the full service can be modified accordingly. All LOCAS customers have individual files held for them and therefore it is possible to choose the type of catalogue, the format and layout of the entries, and the filing order. Output can be on paper, card or COM. LOCAS serves approximately 100 public, academic and special libraries, eg The British Council, British Institute of Recorded Sound, Devon County Library, Ministry of Defence and Sheffield Polytechnic.

Currently, LOCAS is moving from merely a catalogue output system to a filebuilding and maintenance system with derived and original cataloguing. Records can be selected, amended or created online as explained above and this can be facilitated by the use of a microcomputer (a) as a terminal for online access and (b) as a stand-alone machine for processing thus reducing online connect time and telecommunication costs. The procedure is to select the records online and then to download them to the floppy disc store of the micro. They can then be edited using the processing power of the microcomputer, saved in a new file on the floppy discs and then the user can go online again to upload this amended file to the host computer. This CORTEX software runs on a Sirius computer, converted to emulate the appropriate type of terminal and with the keyboard specially adapted with dedicated and function keys. The British Library will maintain a master file or supply a complete file on tape. It is possible, for example, to join LOCAS for a short term in order to build files and then to use the derived tapes as the basis of an in-house system.

Other centralized cataloguing aids

Within the context of centralized cataloguing mention should be made of the many additional services which are available from the Library of Congress and other national libraries, such as authority files, cataloguing notes, filing rules (see also page 92) and user documentation. These and other aids, although they may not always relate specifically to automated cataloguing, are invaluable.

Authority files

The authority file is a source of quality control in that it lists established headings, cross references and other data. The Library of Congress, for instance, maintains an online Name-Authority File, while the British Library provides a similar file on microfiche and also issues a subject authority fiche. The Library of Congress Name-Authority File contains over one million records[1] for personal, corporate, conference, and geographic names and uniform titles. New and retrospectively created records adhere to AACR2 format. This file is available through other networks and individual library systems (eg OCLC — see page 169 — and the Ohio State University Libraries online catalogue). The RLIN network (see page 170) also provides access to the LC file and, in addition, the machine-readable version of Library of Congress *Subject headings* and the New York Public Library's file of names and subjects. The WLN (see page 172) authority file contains three separate types of authority records: authors, series titles, and subjects.

Blackwell North America offers an automated authority control system which can perform name and subject authority control on MARC databases.

Cataloguing in publication

One further very important aspect of the work of the Library of Congress and the British Library is the Cataloguing in

1 *Information bulletin* / Library of Congress 43 (4) January 23 1984

Publication (CIP) programme. The object of this programme is to provide advance information of forthcoming books; cataloguing data being compiled from preliminary matter supplied by various publishers. CIP data is made available through the various centralized services such as MARC tapes and the online databases some time before the projected publication dates of the books described. It also appears in the book itself when published.

A major problem of centralized cataloguing services is currency. The length of time taken from the publication of a book to the appearance of a related full bibliographic record in machine-readable or eye-readable form can be many weeks/ months. From this point of view, the CIP record is so valuable that the British Library intends to extend and monitor more closely its use of this data so that the CIP record may form the actual basis of the 'definitive "national bibliographic" record'.[1] A record will only be revised subsequently if its constituent data change. This is a radical move away from the accepted principle of using the actual item as the primary source of cataloguing data. The non-CIP stream will have lower priority and this may well encourage some of the non-participating publishers to join the scheme.

REMARC
One problem for those libraries who wish to retrospectively convert their catalogues is material for which cataloguing data are not available in the MARC bases. REMARC is a database that may help here. It contains approximately 5 million records of works in the Library of Congress *not* included in MARC. REMARC offers conversion of a library's existing catalogue records into machine-readable form in the MARC format, upgrading them to LC standards. REMARC is a product of Carrollton Press, Arlington, Va, US, and the UK and European agent is Chadwyck-Healey of Cambridge.

Networks
When a number of agencies agree to join together for the purpose of satisfying certain specified cataloguing require-

1 Cataloguing in Publication : the new programme set to take off *British Library Bibliographic Services Division newsletter* (33) April 1984 1-2

ments, then the resultant set-up is referred to as a cataloguing *network*. There could be agreement to share the *cost* or the *work* involved in cataloguing. The former is analogous to the centralized services which have just been described. Such a network can be represented in diagrammatic form thus:

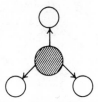

The central database is shown shaded and the direction of flow of the data is indicated by the arrows.

When the work is shared then this may be referred to as *co-operative* cataloguing. The participating institutions both extract data from and input data to the central base:

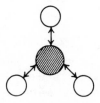

The prime example of co-operative cataloguing is again provided by the Library of Congress in the form of the *National union catalog*. This also originated in 1901 when Herbert Putnam, Librarian of Congress, authorized the exchange of LC cards for those of other libraries. From 1983 the NUC has been produced from a machine-readable base with online input and microfiche output. Currently, there are some 1,500 reporting institutions.

A particular network may, of course, share both the cost *and* the work of cataloguing, paying to receive centrally produced data but inputting in-house data to the system as necessary.

If other features were added to the network, inter-library loans for example, then these links could also be indicated in the network diagram.

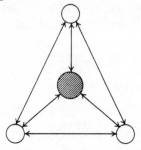

Although the basic constituent operations of networking are not new, the term itself is of comparatively recent origin. This is because it is normally used to refer only to those systems which contain elements of computerization, with machine-readable databases capable of being accessed either on or offline.

A library which opts to join a network may reap the benefit of advantages in terms of:

efficiency
productivity
currency
control
costs

The possible pitfalls of a lengthy 'go-it-alone' development will be avoided and greater efficiency should also be achieved by the economy of sharing, with communal facilities and files requiring a reduced input from the individual library. This in turn means increased productivity. Currency is more problematic but a co-operative effort should, in theory, mean a more up-to-date and comprehensive central database. Centralized cataloguing should also provide better quality and greater consistency and hence control. Shared cataloguing, with input from a number of different agencies can, however, lead to difficulties where quality control is concerned. Whether quality control is affected or not, a further advantage of a co-operative network is the union catalogue which is usually a bi-product.

Costs may not, of course, actually be reduced (due to inflation, etc) but the aim is to reduce the *rate of increase* in cost. Economies of staff may also be realized but this has not always been proved to be the case in practice and, indeed, it can be advantageous to redeploy staff, whenever possible, to tasks which personnel trained in cataloguing can usefully undertake, such as annotation and analysis, advisory work, guiding and display.

All of this sounds very attractive but the paramount concern must be the user. The key question to be asked is: 'Will membership of a network provide an improved *local* service?' Apart from the factors mentioned above, the local catalogue should be:

comprehensive in its coverage
simple to use and to understand
always readily accessible
adaptable to local needs

With regard to comprehensiveness, clearly the larger the central base, the better for the participant, and it must also be possible to create in-house records for material not in this base. Simplicity is a topic of current concern; a network may have an online capability but search 'key' mechanisms and complex screen formats can make this unsuitable for *public* access. Accessibility is also related to the problems which may occur if an automated system 'crashes', ie fails, for some reason, especially if this is an online system. Adaptability requirement will depend upon what the local needs are but, for example, one network may have a single central file accessible to all participants (as OCLC – see page 169), whilst another may permit individual files and greater flexibility (as SWALCAP – see page 180).

Dobrovitz has suggested that the saving of cataloguing costs by accepting centralized cataloguing without regard to local needs, local emphasis, local terminology and local readers may, in the long run, result in a much higher expenditure of *time* by users.[1] Although he was referring to American systems being used in Australian libraries, the inference has general implications.

The network might reduce the rate of increase in costs but some libraries may prefer to stay independent for the attention to local requirement and flexibility which this provides.

1 The future of original cataloguing and the Library of Congress / A. Dobrovitz *Australian library journal* 20 (4) May 1971 16-19

Indeed, De Gennara has maintained that:

> 'One of the hard lessons we are learning from our experience in the 1970's is that cooperation is a difficult, time-consuming, and expensive way to do something, and results are frequently disappointing.'[1]

The principle of shared cataloguing upon which pioneering networks such as OCLC were originally based has therefore become less sacrosanct in recent years as the competition from other services which attempt to cater more specifically for local needs has increased:

> 'The interest, energy and resources that went into network building in the 1970's are now going into buying, and installing mini- and microcomputer-based local systems with particular emphasis on the local online catalog and retrospective conversion.'[2]

Of course, as De Gennaro points out, there is little doubt that these local systems will eventually acquire the capability to link with each other (and with other networks) for shared cataloguing and other purposes. Thus the spirit of co-operation will not die; the network will live on albeit in a rather different form.

To sum up, membership of a network can bring with it considerable benefits but it may also pose certain problems with regard to local user needs and the service provided may not live up to local expectations.

There are now a number of networks to select from, many of which are moving towards a more local and distributive system, and some of these will be described in more detail in the next chapter.

Combinations

From the detail supplied above, it becomes apparent that a combination of options can be a very useful and realistic proposition. The library which goes its own way might still find it beneficial to subscribe to the MARC service. A public library in the UK could expect to find cataloguing data for upwards of 80% of its additions to stock already available in MARC format. For academic libraries the

1 Library automation & networking perspectives on three decades / Richard De Gennaro *Library journal* 108 (7) April 1 1983 629-635
2 *ibid.*

percentage would be considerably lower but still of useful proportions.

It has already been indicated that tailor-made systems such as Geac are MARC compatible and it is therefore possible to combine an independent system of this nature with a centralized MARC service.

Centralized services such as LOCAS are built around the MARC databases.

Progressing a stage further, it would be economically short-sighted, to say the least, for a large co-operative network such as OCLC in the United States or BLCMP in the UK, *not* to take advantage of the MARC service. This is obviously a very attractive proposition, with the centralized MARC bases being supplemented by the co-operative and combined input of a number of libraries. The network, however, may find it difficult to cater for local needs as efficiently as the package created specifically for an individual library.

The current trend therefore appears to be for the two major areas of development, ie (1) the individual library oriented turnkey package and (2) the co-operative network, to move more closely into line. More packages now incorporate MARC compatibility so that centralized cataloguing services can be utilized and the networks perceive the advantages of local processing based on mini or microcomputers.

A further possibility is for a library to make use of a co-operative service for its general cataloguing requirements and an in-house system for other purposes. For example, Liverpool Polytechnic library is a member of the SWALCAP network (see page 180) but the cataloguing terminals are also linked to the Polytechnic's DEC-20 mainframe, which is used for the maintenance of small specialized databases, eg audiovisual material, and for electronic mail, etc.

Retrospective conversion
As pointed out earlier, a major problem for libraries which automate their catalogues is the retrospective conversion of existing manual records. This could take many years and prove quite costly. In the meantime, multiple catalogues, the 'closed' manual and the new automated, must be maintained. There is no complete ready made 'ideal' answer and many libraries have to live with this situation. Use can be made of the MARC bases and useful services such as REMARC

(see page 150) are available but local data must still be added and this in itself can be very time consuming. A further possibility is the employment of 'cheap' labour to undertake the task. For example, in the UK, manpower made available under employment schemes run by central government (the Manpower Services Commission) is sometimes utilized.

Considerable help may be available, at a price, if the library subscribes to a network utility. OCLC (see page 169), for example, offers such a service. Conversion is direct from card or other files, including the entry of local data, using shifts of operators at multiple terminals. Tens of thousands of records per week can be handled in this way.

If the catalogue is already automated when a library implements a new system then conversion will obviously be easier although difficulties will still be encountered. Programs can be written to automatically convert and, if necessary, upgrade records. When Liverpool Polytechnic joined the SWALCAP (see page 180) network, for instance, the Systems Librarian (Graham Chan) wrote the necessary programs to convert the previous in-house machine-readable records into the MARC format. Similar work has been undertaken at other institutions and the networks themselves can provide assistance in this area.

For libraries that do not have access to bibliographic networks, a system called MITINET/retro (pronounced 'mighty-net') has been developed in the US. This supports retrospective conversion for small and medium sized libraries allowing the conversion of catalogue records into machine-readable tapes in the MARC format. It requires a microfiche reader and an Apple II Plus or Apple IIe microcomputer with 48K of storage and one floppy disc drive.[1]

Integration

It is the author's view that any consideration given to the automation of the cataloguing process should not be undertaken in a vacuum. Processes which are closely linked to cataloguing or which use the catalogue as a source file should also be considered at the same time so that eventually, if not immediately, an integrated ordering, cataloguing, circulation control, etc system may be implemented.

1 MITINET/retro : retrospective conversion on an Apple / Hank Epstein *Information technology and libraries* 2 (2) June 1983 166-168

'An integrated system has positive benefits for libraries since an expensive "fixed" resource — the computer, disc drives, and software — is being utilized for several functions; hence the costs for each function decline.'[1]

The importance of integration is recognized by the networks and by commercial turnkey package suppliers. The overall design of the famed OCLC system (see page 169) provides for an integrated, comprehensive, online system and includes amongst its features acquisitions, cataloguing, serials handling, circulation control and interlibrary loan. Turnkey packages previously mentioned in this work, such as CLSI, Dataphase, Geac and Urica, are used as the basis for integrated systems. Geac offers a 'total' solution to a library's needs, including acquisition, cataloguing, circulation and statistical information as individual options or as a complete package. Another commercial offering, the Telepen-LMR library system, claims to provide the answer for those libraries who have argued the case for total integration within one system of all of a library's many functions. The system includes book ordering, cataloguing, circulation control, word processing (to assist administration) and information retrieval, including SDI (Selective Dissemination of Information) and current awareness.

Most of the public online catalogues in the United States have been planned as part of a larger integrated library system.[2]

In the UK, apart from networks and packages such as OCLC and Geac which are mentioned above, other networks, eg BLCMP (see page 178) and commercial services, eg Oriel, do not confine their activities to cataloguing but cater for other operations such as circulation control.

Some systems, which are basically circulation control systems, offer an online search facility which may be used as a substitute, or even an alternative 'catalogue', albeit one which is for staff use only. An example is ALS (Automated Library Systems — see following page).

The integration factor provides a further indication of the close link which exists between cataloguing and the 'index-

1 Competition & change : the 1983 automated library system marketplace / Joseph R. Matthews *op. cit.*
2 Online public access to library files in North America / Alan Seal *op. cit.*

```
SELECT
  KEY
  -
  1    STOP BORROWER
  2    FREE BORROWER
  3    TEST BORROWER
  4    MAKE RESERVATION
  5    CANCEL RESERVATION
  6    TEST RESERVATION
  7    BORROWER ACTION
  8    BOOK ACTION
  9    ISSUE
  0    RETURN
  :    RENEW
  -    IDENTIFY
```

┌─────────────────┐
│   Screen 1   │
│   │
│ Select IDENTIFY │
└─────────────────┘

```
IDENTIFY          KEY
    ALSN C          0
    CONN            1
    ATKEY           2
    TKEY   WAROWORL 3

    BRWR B          5
    BKEY            6

DISPOSAL

    GP/PG           9
    PRTGP           X
    RESUME          8
```

┌─────────────┐
│ Screen 2   │
│   │
│ Identify   │
│ Title KEY   │
└─────────────┘

┌──────────────┐
│ Screen 3   │
│   │
│ Detail of   │
│   first   │
│ relevant   │
│   item   │
└──────────────┘

```
IDENTIFY TKEY WAROWORL SYN 001
         CONN  0 71100062 X
MASTER ALSN  C 05455623 8

TAYLOR, JOHN WILLIAM RANSOM WA
RPLANES OF THE WORLD, COMPLETE
LY REVISED AND UPDATED  2ND ED
.  ALLAN, 1968 (I.E. 1969).
ATKEY  TAYJWOWO
TKEY   WAROWORL
CLASSIFICATION  623.746
BOOK TYPE  ANF
CATEGORY
RELATED CONN 0 00000000 0
COPIES  0002  RESERVATIONS 000
```

*Online searching using a 'title key' at Cheshire Libraries.
This system (ALS) is basically a circulation control system
but offers an online search capability for book details (staff
access only)*

ing and abstracting' type of database. MEDLARS, for example, is in process of developing a completely integrated service with ordering, acquisition, base work, information retrieval, cataloguing, document delivery, indexing, inventory control and management facilities. This will be based on a relational database management system.

More about costs

Financial implications obviously constitute a major management factor but, unfortunately, this is something about which it is difficult to draw precise conclusions and make detailed recommendations, particularly in relation to the cost-benefits to be gained over the existing catalogue.

From the various indications provided throughout this text, it should be clear that, dependent upon requirement and available resources, the cost of an automated system may vary from as low as a few thousand pounds for a microcomputer and appropriate software to some hundreds of thousands of pounds for a mainframe system.

The Cheshire Educational Resources Library installed a microcomputer system for under £10,000 which will handle up to 50,000 records, each of 250 characters, to be stored on hard disc and made available in-house online via multiple terminals.

Liverpool Polytechnic Library, when it joined the SWAL-CAP network (see page 180), incurred capital costs of approximately £36,000, which included a minicomputer (£9,000), multiple vdu's (£8,750), enhancement to the Polytechnic's computer communication system (£7,000) and a printer (£700). The remaining £10,750 was for telecommunication charges (ie modem, line installation and local wiring).

In addition to capital costs, recurring and maintenance costs must be taken into account and these can be high. Liverpool Polytechnic Library's estimated revenue for this purpose (1984-5) is £41,775, which includes equipment maintenance, telecommunication charges, processing and online transaction charges and COM production charges.

Seal estimates that present prices for an effective integrated system, offering online public access and other modules for operations such as circulation control, etc are at least £80-100,000 and up to £300,000 for a large library.[1] The lower end of this price range could fall in the next few years to about £40,000 in current terms for a complete hardware/software package.

It has been suggested that public access online catalogues will in the long run become cheaper than COM output.[2] Some libraries are already finding that the cost of producing a completely updated COM catalogue every month is becoming excessive.[3] At the Polytechnic of North London, for instance, 'the microfiche catalogue, produced in 35 copies each month completely superseding the previous issue, has reached a size and cost that is alarming.'[4] Two possible solutions are: (1) to lessen the frequency of production, or (2) to reduce the amount of detail in the entries. The Polytechnic of North London, as a member of BLCMP (see page 178), and in common with other COM catalogue producers, is planning to go online. Of course, the initial cost of computer terminals will be much more than COM readers and will comprise a major element of expenditure. It is difficult to calculate the number of terminals that will be required; one estimate is one terminal per 100 daily users.[5] Terminals will be required for both staff and public use. The University of Hull, for example, has a total of twenty terminals but only seven are presently used for public access.[6]

Other items of expenditure may also have to be considered such as those involved in data preparation, conversion and input. There is, in addition, where an online public access catalogue is concerned, the possible expense of a back-up system.

1 The development of online catalogues / Alan Seal *In Introducing the online catalogue : papers based on seminars held in 1983* / edited by Alan Seal. — Bath University Library Centre for Catalogue Research, 1984
2 *The future of the catalog : the library's choices* / S. Michael Malinconico and Paul J. Fasana. — Knowledge Industry Publications, 1979 85-86
2 The development of online catalogues / Alan Seal *op. cit.* 4
3 Management problems arising from the introduction of automation / Simon Francis *The electronic library* 2 (1) January 1984 25-29
4 The library catalog : COM and online options *Library technology reports* 16 (5) 505
5 Online public access catalogues : experiences at the University of Hull / Tom Graham *In* Introducing the online catalogue / edited by Alan Seal *op. cit.* 22

Effect of automation on staff

One aspect of cataloguing management that cannot be overlooked is the impact of increasing automation on library staff. In Norway, the relevant trade union has been interested in finding out what effect computerization has had on personnel. Although Norway is perhaps under-developed in terms of automation, this was, nevertheless, an interesting study. After interviewing staff who had recently experienced automation in their libraries, one of the major findings was that adequate training is a very important requisite. This training should include participation and communication as the system develops. A general understanding of how the computer works was considered to be essential.[1]

Perry, writing about the online public catalogue, also maintains that training is of fundamental importance: 'The vendor should provide quite extensive training: typically one or two members of the library staff will receive training and become expert in operating the system and actually using it: they will then assume responsibility for training other members of staff ... The library will also find it useful to have a test or training database, ie a small file separate from the normal file, which can be used for training purposes and also for demonstrations to visitors without jeopardizing the live system.'[2]

Jagodzinski stresses the significance of staff reactions to computers now that staff who are completely untrained in computing are being asked to operate computer terminals as part of their daily routine. If early experiences are unfavourable then staff will avoid using a system as much as possible and it will be deemed a failure.[3]

Attempts should be made to allay the fears that are often based on false information. These might include the fear that there is a need for scientific or mathematical knowledge, the fear that there are health risks attached to the continual use of a vdu, or even the fear of redundancy.

Where employment is concerned, it is probable that in the

1 Address to students of the School of Librarianship and Information Studies Liverpool Polytechnic by Ragnar Nordlie in May 1983
2 The implementation of an online public catalogue / Niall Perry *op. cit.*
3 Staff attitudes to computers / Peter Jagodzinski *Vine* (41) December 1981 36-39

initial stages of automation more rather than less staff will be required and the computer may well, at a later stage, open up new tasks and new opportunities. One of the greatest advantages of the computer is that it can eliminate those routine tasks which give less job satisfaction, eg filing, and provide more time for those more enjoyable 'book' and 'information' based activities.

'Automation has not meant, as many library administrators once hoped, a reduction in personnel (except, of course, where automation has resulted in a tightening of workflow patterns and a more efficient use of personnel); instead, the chief staffing change has been an increase in the responsibilities of clericals and paraprofessionals and often an upgrading of positions . . . A large percentage of what was once considered original cataloging in many libraries is now being handled at computer terminals by support staff who must be knowledgeable in MARC formats, the latest cataloging code, and local cataloging practices.'[1]

The cataloguer should be encouraged to accept the challenge of the computer and enabled to use it as a powerful ally in the provision of a more effective service. In order that this may be done, it is most important that computerized systems are designed to be as user-friendly as possible.

Preparing and training the user

This is a most essential aspect of any computerized project. The user should be informed at an early stage that a new system is to be introduced and kept informed of its progress. This is obviously a useful publicity exercise and will foster good customer relations. Details of how the system will operate should be provided and any expected improvements in the library service described. If the user will be required to operate equipment, as with a COM or online catalogue, then he/she should be given some indication of what will be required and reassured as to the ease with which the equipment may be used. Adequate verbal and printed advice and instruction should be available when the system is finally launched. With an interactive online system, there may well be additional integral 'help' features and 'tutorial' instruction facilities.

1 *Managing the catalog department* / Donald L. Foster. — 2nd ed. — Scarecrow Press, 1982 97-98

Perry stresses the need for a manifest enthusiasm on the part of the staff which will, hopefully, be conveyed to the user.[1]

Installing and testing the system

Whatever the chosen option, there will almost certainly be teething troubles. Patience, calmness and clear thinking must be the virtues to aspire to in such circumstances. The number and seriousness of the problems will depend on the size and complexity of the system but Perry, from his experiences with SCOLCAP as a customer and with OCLC as a supplier and installer of systems, succinctly paints a picture of what might happen:

'Installing and testing the system is quite likely to be a painful affair. The library will very likely end up wondering what prompted it to buy the system in the first place! The processor will fail, and the terminals will fail. If you are lucky this will not happen all at once! The vendor's engineers will grow irritable unless you care for them. They are doing a complex job so if you pamper them you will find that they respond better. It will be difficult, but the library must reserve judgment on the system, or the vendor, or his staff, until the system has been actually accepted and is under warranty. At all costs avoid acrimony. This may be obvious but circumstances do arise that will test the patience of a saint; those are the times to keep plugging on until a solution is found.'[2]

---

1 The implementation of an online public catalogue / Niall Perry *op. cit.*
2 The implementation of an online public catalogue / Niall Perry *op. cit.* 42

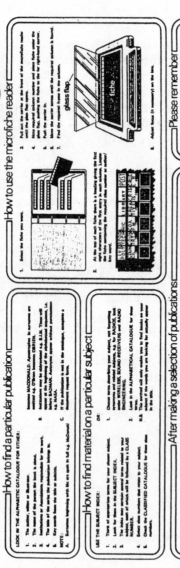

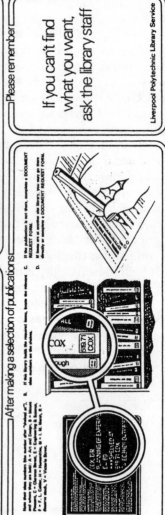

Instructions for using the computer produced microfiche catalogue. Liverpool Polytechnic Library. Actual size: 12 × 16 in.

SEARCHING ON HERMES

TERMINAL SEARCHING

The terminals are left on continuously and SHOULD NOT BE SWITCHED OFF. Instructions are displayed on the screen in a logical sequence. They are self-explanatory and require no special knowledge to use. After entering your selection, always press SEND to communicate with the computer. To return to the first screen to begin a search, enter X followed by SEND. To correct an error, simply backspace. Filing is alphabetical, letter by letter. Numbers and letters — but not spaces or punctuation — are read, except in the call number, where the period is read also.

FEATURES OF THE SYSTEM

- **Searching by AUTHOR:** Enter the author's name as follows:

    SMITH RICHARD C

    or   SMITH R C

    The system will respond with five entries on the screen, with the nearest match in the middle. SMITH R C will appear before SMITH RICHARD C. Browse forward and backward in the file to cover all possibilities.

- **Searching by TITLE:** Enter as much of the title as is necessary to identify the book. Since filing is alphabetic with all articles ignored (except "a" and "il"), it doesn't matter if you enter THE MAGUS or just MAGUS. Titles starting with a number file before alphabetic entries. Depending on how a title was catalogued you might find an item under 8080 MICROCOMPUTER EXPERIMENTS or EIGHTY EIGHTY MICROCOMPUTER EXPERIMENTS. Search under both forms. Series titles are not included in HERMES

FOR A MORE EFFICIENT SEARCH, ALWAYS SEARCH UNDER BOTH TITLE AND AUTHOR.

Extracts from the instructions for using public online catalogue at the University of Ottawa. In this case, Canada being a bi-lingual country, instructions (both hardcopy and on vdu) are also available in French. (Publicity material at the University of Ottawa is currently (September 1984) in process of revision.)

ULP 17.21
(1984)

Glasgow University Library

WELCOME TO THE ONLINE CATALOGUE!

Catalogue 1 is now online. It contains most of the books you are likely to want, and offers you more choice in how to look for them.

The online catalogue is easy to use. Instructions on the screen will guide you at all stages, so experiment with it as much as you like!

As you explore its possibilities, please let us have your comments and suggestions for further improvement.

USING THE ONLINE CATALOGUE

PRESS 'CLEAR' to start

FOLLOW INSTRUCTIONS on the screen

The 'SEND' key is the large red key

PRESS 'HELP' at any time, and additional guidance will be displayed

PRESS 'QUICK SEARCH' to look at instructions for a time-saving way of using the catalogue

PRESS 'CLEAR' when you leave the terminal.

Other useful keys:

CAT: *To start a new search without going back to the very beginning*

PREVIOUS SCREEN: *To display again the screen or screens you have just seen*

TIL: *To start a new Title search, or to switch from e.g. Author to Title search*

AUT: *To start a new Author search, or to switch from e.g. Keyword to Author search*

KEY: *To start a new Keyword search, or to switch from e.g. Title to Keyword search.*

REMEMBER that many of the Library's older books are still only listed in Catalogue 2 and Catalogue 3.

The Reading Room and Departmental Libraries also have more books than those listed in the online catalogue.

IF IN DOUBT ASK LIBRARY STAFF!

Glasgow University Library (UK) instruction sheet for using the online catalogue

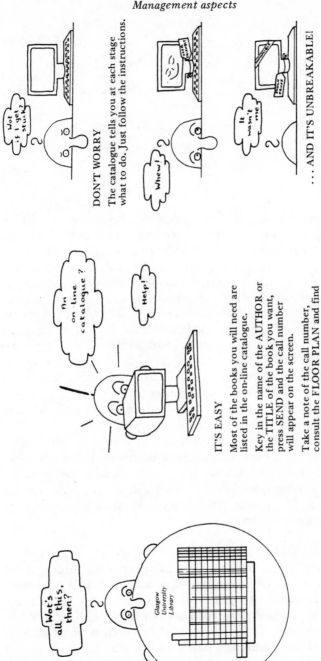

Glasgow University Library. Extracts from a leaflet issued to freshers (to entice rather than to instruct)

Chapter Nine

Networks

Before considering specific network developments, it is necessary to reiterate one or two important general points.

It should be noted, first of all, that there is a difference between an online cataloguing facility and an online public access catalogue. It is possible, in many network systems, to enter a centralized database online, to call up a record, to amend that record to suit the individual library's requirement and then to add the amended record to the library's master file. The online search facility and output screen formats, however, may not be suitable for public use. Online access is therefore restricted to staff and the final public catalogue output will be in COM or some other form.

Secondly, the multi-user nature of a network system makes it difficult to cater for local individual needs.

The current trend therefore, accelerated by the competition from commercial turnkey packages, is for networks to work towards distributive, local stand-alone systems using minicomputers. Such systems will usually cater for the integration of various related activities such as cataloguing and circulation control.

The United States
The United States led the world in networking; bibliographic utilities such as OCLC and services such as MEDLARS were the forerunners of many other systems. As regards the former, the major networks are OCLC, RLIN and WLN. The University of Toronto's UTLAS system must also be considered for, although based in Canada, its products are also available in the US.

The utilities are similar in many respects; all offer cataloguing services; all include MARC records in their databases. However, there are differences, for example not all utilities currently have a subject search facility. The first computerized cataloguing network, the pacemaker for those that were to follow, was OCLC.

OCLC Online Computer Library Center Inc

OCLC is a non-profit making organization based in Dublin, (previously Columbus), Ohio, which operates an online library system for academic, public and special libraries. Established in 1967 as the Ohio College Library Center, the first computerized service became operational in 1970, with a batch-processed MARC-based monograph cataloguing system. This was replaced in 1971 by an online remote access system which led to considerable expansion. The organization changed its name to OCLC, Inc in 1977 to reflect nationwide growth from 54 Ohio libraries to upwards of 2,500 libraries all over the United States and Canada. The name was changed again in 1981. Today, overseas libraries are part of the system. There is an OCLC Europe located in Birmingham, England. The first libraries in the UK to become subscribers were the Universities of Essex and Newcastle in 1981.

To achieve its basic objectives, ie to increase availability of library resources for users of participating libraries, and to reduce the rate of rise of per-unit costs in libraries, OCLC has created a computer network system in which over 4,000 specially designed vdu terminals are linked to the OCLC computer in Ohio by dedicated telephone lines. Other members use dial-access terminals.

Users of these terminals have at their fingertips an online file of information containing details of well over nine million books and other library materials, including serials, audiovisual items, manuscripts, maps, music scores and sound recordings.

As noted earlier, OCLC, in common with the other utilities, is moving towards a more distributive and local service. A Selective Record Service (SDS) is now available which allows libraries to extract and make use of OCLC cataloguing information without requiring any input in return. OCLC has also developed jointly with Online Computers Inc the latter's ILS (Integrated Library System — which was developed in the first instance by the National Library of Medicine).

This provides for a package of five subsystems: Administrative, Bibliographic, Catalogue Access, Circulation and Serials.[1] In addition, OCLC has purchased Avatar, the only other commercial company marketing ILS.[2] The online cataloguing subsystem permits access via author, title, subject (ie 'keyword') and certain other defined access points. One US library has a further 15 types of search on offer.[3]

A new OCLC M300 Workstation is supplied by IBM and is based upon the IBM Personal Computer. This has provided the opportunity to make the OCLC services even more cost-effective and convenient and is another indicator of OCLC's commitment to distributive systems. OCLC is also looking toward additional microcomputer software that could be of value to OCLC members.[4]

One of the major drawing cards of OCLC continues to be its size in terms of the number of records in the central online union catalogue, the largest database of its kind in the world. In the UK, the University of Newcastle, which will shortly (late 1984/early 1985) be providing online public access to its catalogues via the ILS (LS/2000) system, cites a cataloguing 'hit rate' of upwards of 90%. In December 1982, OCLC decided to copyright its database, claiming that this action recognized the growing value to the information community of this unique international resource.[5]

RLIN (Research Libraries Information Network)

RLIN, like OCLC, is also nationwide in scope. The RLG (Research Libraries Group), which is responsible for RLIN, is a consortium of research libraries dedicated to resolving common problems in collection development, management, access and preservation. The network can provide members with online catalogues and automated acquisition and inter-library loan systems.

1 OCLC's local system and a new selective records service / David Buckle and N. Perry *Vine* (49) August 1983 19-25
2 Online public access to library files in North America / Alan Seal *op. cit.*
3 *ibid.*
4 *Introducing the M300.* — OCLC. Publicity leaflet 1984
5 Library networking in the United States, 1982 / Glyn T. Evans *The Bowker annual of library & book trade information.* — 28th ed. — Bowker, 1983 70-76

The OCLC M300 Workstation, an IBM Personal Computer to which OCLC has added special hardware and software features to allow the OCLC Online System to be accessed. (The screen format displayed here is similar to that shown on page 97)

In early 1978 RLG announced its intention to utilize BALLOTS (Bibliographic Automation of Large Library Operations using a Timesharing System), which was based on Stanford University in California. BALLOTS is an online system combining some of the features of OCLC, some of Lockheed/SDC (see page 176) and some features not available on either of the other two systems. It has a subject capability; searches can be made using classification numbers and subject headings.

When it became the system selected by RLG, BALLOTS adopted the name RLIN. Currently, the RLIN network 'serves fewer users and supports fewer terminals than OCLC but its subject search capability and the other selective databases available cause a heavy demand on the system.'[1] The

1 Library networking in the United States, 1982 / Glyn T. Evans *op. cit.*

recently developed RLIN Reports System (RRS) caters for
the preparation of bibliographic lists from MARC records
selected online.[1]

Like OCLC, RLIN is moving towards a distributive service.
In 1982 RLG announced the receipt of a grant of $250,000
to begin research on such a system.[2]

WLN (Washington Library Network)
WLN dates back to 1967 when the Washington State Library
assumed responsibility for developing the network. Ten libraries
participated in a batch pilot system in 1972 and an 'early' online system was developed in 1975. By 1977, WLN computer
services were being made available to libraries outside the
State of Washington. At present WLN has 120 participants,
geographically dispersed between Arizona and Alaska.[3]

WLN provides its members with shared cataloguing and
catalogue maintenance, including retrospective conversion.
An automated acquisitions facility is also offered. The
central database consists of approximately three million
bibliographic records. WLN is still essentially a regional
cataloguing system but its software includes sophisticated
online searching and authority control.[4]

In common with other utilities, WLN believes that libraries
will benefit from the increased local processing capability
that micro and minicomputers can provide and as from 1984
participants are offered a modified IBM personal computer as
an alternative to the previous Hazeltine terminals. This change
marks WLN's move into both microcomputers and distributed processing.[5]

Other networks of the US
Although space does not permit a detailed examination,
mention should be made of the other regional organizations

1 The RLIN Reports System : a tool for MARC selection and listing /
Walt Crawford *Information technology and libraries* 3 (1) March 1984
3-14
2 Library networking in the United States, 1982 / Glyn T. Evans *op.
cit.*
3 The WLN PC : local processing in a network context / David Andresen
Information technology and libraries 3 (1) March 1984 54-58
4 Online public access to library files in North America / Alan Seal *op.
cit.*
5 The WLN PC / David Andresen *op. cit.*

many of which currently depend upon utilities such as OCLC for their computerized services. Examples are CAPCON (Washington, DC), NELINET (New England Library Network) and SOLINET (South Eastern Library Network). The latter makes use of WLN software for its regional union catalogue.[1]

One or two networks have decided to end their affiliation to OCLC, eg MIDLNET (Midwest Regional Library Network) in 1983, and phase out this segment of their operations, the libraries joining other regional networks.[2]

Conversely there has been a trend with OCLC toward the strengthening of relationships with regional networks. 'Given the wide range of missions, interests, and structures that exist among the networks, this is not an insignificant development.'[3]

The role of the Library of Congress and the Network Advisory Committee

It was probably inevitable, if perhaps unfortunate, that network progress, in the context of the bibliographic utilities, should have been made in a piecemeal way with no overall national system. However, the Library of Congress has assumed the role of 'co-ordinator'.

LC's involvement in networking goes back a long way. As previously indicated, it began a card service in 1901 and, more recently, began work on the MARC project and the subsequent MARC Distribution Service in 1965. In the mid-1970s, LC responded to a suggestion that it should assume the role of network co-ordinator by establishing a Network Development Office and by calling the first meeting of the Network Advisory Committee in 1976. Representatives of the major network organizations were invited to attend this meeting to discuss networking activities and to explore ways in which a more cohesive nationwide system might be developed. A preliminary edition of the Committee's first planning paper was published in 1977.[4]

1 Online public access to library files in North America / Alan Seal *op. cit.*

2 Library networking in the United States, 1982 / Glyn T. Evans *op. cit.*

3 *ibid.*

4 *Towards a national library and information science network : the library bibliographic component* / Network Advisory Group. — Prelim. ed. — Library of Congress, 1977. (The Network Advisory Group changed its name to the Network Advisory Committee in 1977)

A study commissioned by the Network Development Office and funded by NCLIS (National Commission on Libraries and Information Science) was published in 1978[1] and this supported LC's role as coordinator and stated that the requirement for machine-readable records would be largely satisfied if LC continued and expanded its MARC services and made the data available both on and offline.

The Library of Congress began to establish a core bibliographic base for a national system, using MARC as a cornerstone, in 1969. By early 1984 the MARC (Books) database had grown to over one and three quarter million records.[2] It is increasing by 110 thousand records annually. Within LC, there have been several automation projects designed to facilitate access to and manipulation of this base. These include MUMS (MUltiple Use MARC System) for online interrogation and correction of MARC data; APIF (Automated Process Information File), which is designed to determine whether an item is in stock and to speed up and improve processing techniques; and SCORPIO (Subject Content Oriented Retriever for Processing Information Online), which is a general purpose retrieval system designed for use with MARC databases and other files.

MARC bibliographic record distribution services are handled by the Cataloguing Distribution Service of LC. 'The growth of local processing does not seem to be lessening the dependence of American libraries on LC cataloguing.'[3]

The Library has also participated in two co-operative programmes for the conversion of printed records to machine-readable form. COMARC (COoperative MARC) is an attempt to share the effort of converting bibliographic data relating to monographs; the resultant records being distributed without charge to participating libraries. CONSER (CONversion of SERials) aims at the creation of a national machine-readable database of quality serials cataloguing information. A number of libraries with extensive serial collections co-operate in the project and records are input directly to the OCLC database. The Library of Congress and the National

1 *The role of the Library of Congress in the evolving national network* / Lawrence F. Buckland. — Library of Congress, 1978
2 *Information bulletin* / Library of Congress 43 (4) January 23 1984 15
3 Online public access to library files in North America / Alan Seal *op. cit.*

Library of Canada act as authentication centres. A final projected total of some 200,000 to 300,000 serial records is intended.

The Name-Authority base (see also page 149) has also been a partially co-operative effort. Nearly 100,000 records have been submitted by participants in the Name Authority Cooperative (NACO) project.

In 1981, LC, with funding from the Council on Library Resources, joined forces with the Research Libraries Group and the Washington Library Network (see also page 172) to develop an online communications link and an intersystem data retrieval and maintenance facility to support a shared authority file. This Linked Systems Project will allow later sharing of full cataloguing records, location and holdings data. This is a welcome move towards a national network based upon a diversity of systems linked by a standard interface.

As well as monitoring the LC's national MARC services, the Network Development Office continues to analyse the Library's role in the international exchange of MARC records. As noted on page 39 specifications for the conversion of records in the US MARC format into the UNIMARC format have been prepared and MARC data in the UNIMARC format distributed. British MARC records are also converted into the US MARC format and are available through the MARC Distribution Service.

Indexing and abstracting services
The central databases of networks such as OCLC and RLIN consist of records of documents. There are other networks, eg MEDLARS, which provide records of the *contents* of such documents. The latter is analogous to analytical cataloguing. A detailed discussion of these bases is outside the scope of this text but nevertheless they cannot be completely ignored in the computerized cataloguing context for they require similar indexing techniques and the end result of searching in them is similar to the result of searching a catalogue — the production of a bibliographic citation or citations.

MEDLARS (MEDical Literature Analysis and Retrieval System)/MEDLINE
In common with many other databases, MEDLARS was primarily an offshoot from a printed indexing service. The

database, which contains references from some 3,000 bio-medical journals published throughout the world, is the same as that used to create *Index medicus* and *International nursing index*.

At first, such databases were 'batch' processed; that is, an enquiry was sent off, processed, and two to three weeks later a computer print-out listing relevant references would be received by the enquirer. He or she could then obtain copies of required articles through the usual library channels.

Now, however, the MEDLARS service, which is provided by the National Library of Medicine (US), is online (MEDLINE) and is arguably the world's foremost database of its type.

There are now a great many online 'indexing and abstracting' services of which MEDLARS was the pioneer. Here are just a few examples:

COMPENDEX (COMPuterized ENgineering inDEX)
Abstracted information from the world's significant engineering and technological literature.

ERIC (Educational Resources Information Center)
File of educational materials: research projects, projects, and journal articles.

NTIS (National Technical Information Service)
Database consisting of government-sponsored research, development, and engineering plus analyses prepared by federal agencies and others.

PSYCHINFO (formerly Psychological abstracts)
Psychology and related social science areas.

Dialog and SDC

At one time, databases were accessed separately but subsequently large networks of bases such as those first introduced by Lockheed (now Dialog Information Services, Inc) and the System Development Corporation (SDC), with its ORBIT retrieval system, were set up in an attempt to standardize access languages. Unfortunately, these two organizations went their own individual ways and the result was that there are now two major access programs. However, each of these programs provides one search methodology for accessing a large number of databases and this makes the job of the searcher considerably easier. Once having got into the system, he or she can switch from database to database at will. The databases in the Dialog system, for example, number upwards of 180 (January 1984) and contain in excess of 80 million records.

Such networks contain not only databases of the abstracting and indexing type but also some others. Dialog, for instance, provides access to bibliographic files such as LCMARC and REMARC. SDC has LIBCON which also contains LCMARC records.

In addition, there are now a number of non-bibliographic bases which provide actual information rather than references to sources. Examples are:

EIS INDUSTRIAL PLANTS

Answers a broad range of questions concerning the US industrial economy.

US EXPORTS

Gives export statistics for all commodities in dollar values and shipping weight.

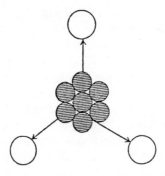

Diagram of the Dialog type of network with a number of databases in the nucleus

Networks of the United Kingdom

Although the UK tended to lag behind the US in the development of online networks, there have, in recent years, been some major developments on a national and regional scale.

BLAISE (British Library Automated Information Service)

BLAISE became operational in early 1977 and has since established itself as one of the world's largest services. Using a combination of online and offline computer processing techniques BLAISE has two major functions: (1) the provision of an automated information retrieval service; (2) the facilitation of library housekeeping from catalogue production through to inter-library loans.

With regard to (1), BLAISE-LINK concentrates on a group of authoritative subject-related files 'not available as a collection from any other single source.'[1] It is operated in collaboration with the National Library of Medicine (US) and the available bases include, for instance, MEDLINE, CANCER-LINE (for cancer specialists) and HEALTH (for non-clinical aspects of health-care). Other files, eg CATLINE, SERLINE and NAF (Name Authority File), provide records of books and serials held by the NLM and an authority check on the form of names used in NLM catalogues. BLAISE-LINE provides information retrieval and cataloguing data in all subject areas. The databases available via this service include: UK MARC (1950 to date); LC MARC (1968 to date); AV-MARC (bibliographic records of non-book materials with particular emphasis on audiovisual materials used for teaching purposes); British Education Index (records of journal articles and conference proceedings); Conference Proceedings Index; and ESTC (Eighteenth Century Short Title Catalogue — an international project to produce a machine-readable short-title catalogue of books, pamphlets and ephemera printed in the eighteenth century).

At present, BLAISE-LINE is a base-switching system, ie different files have to be asked for as required. A projected BLAISE-LINE 2 will be more user-friendly and will appear, to the user at least, as a single integrated file.

An important part of BLAISE is LOCAS which was described on page 148.

BLCMP (Library Services) Ltd

BLCMP began life in 1969 as the Birmingham Libraries Cooperative Mechanization Project. The first co-operative automated cataloguing service in the UK, its membership consisted originally of three libraries only (the Universities of Aston and Birmingham and Birmingham Public Libraries). These three libraries were joined later by Birmingham Polytechnic, and there are now (1984) 37 members from various

1 *How BLAISE-LINK can help you* BLAISE publicity leaflet, 1984

BLAISE-LINE BASIC FEATURES

GING IN

- THROUGH THE BLAISE NETWORK

Dial nearest node in Network (having checked the terminal settings).

On hearing whistling tone connect to acoustic coupler or press DATA button on modem.

Type upper case letter O, press carriage return key.

System will respond

PLEASE ENTER /LOGIN

Type /LOGIN and carriage return.

System will prompt

PLEASE ENTER USERID/PASSWORD

Wait for 3 lines of masking to print and then enter your USERID and password separated by a slash.

- THROUGH PSS (UK Users only)

Dial nearest PSS node (having checked the terminal settings).

On hearing whistling tone connect the acoustic coupler or press DATA button on modem.

Press carriage return twice, type A2, and press carriage return once more.

System will respond with the line number.

Enter your own Network User Identifier (NUI), a hyphen, and press carriage return.

After the ADD? prompt enter the BLAISE-LINE Network User Address A219200222 followed by carriage return.

System will respond

234219200222+COM

Type /LOGIN and press carriage return.

System will prompt

PLEASE ENTER USERID/PASSWORD

0. Wait for 3 lines of masking to print and then enter your USERID and password separated by a slash.

CHANGING FILES

To change files at any time enter FILE, one space and the name, or abbreviated name, of any BLAISE-LINE file.

FILE BEI

SEARCHING

Enter your search term(s) after any SS n/C? and USER: prompt. Remember to use search qualifiers or type the word ALL in front of each term.

SS 1 /C?
USER:
ALL GARDEN AND ALL ENGLISH
PROG:
SS (1) PSTG (194)

This search found 194 records.

SELECTING SEARCH TERMS

Use the NBR command to view the online index of search terms.

NBR GARDEN

COMBINING SEARCH TERMS

Terms can be combined using the logical operators AND, OR and AND NOT.

(TW) HEAT OR HOT

This will search for the words HEAT or HOT in the title field.

TRUNCATION

:   colon stands for no character, a space or several characters in the middle or end of a term.

hash stands for one character or a space in the middle or end of a term.

PRINTING

To view the results of your search online or print the records offline, enter the PRT command after any USER: cue.

LOGGING OFF

Type STOP Y and press carriage return to log off at any time.

April 1984

Printed guide to the basic features of BLAISE-LINE

parts of the UK (eg Guildhall School of Music and Drama, Warwickshire County Libraries and Ulster Polytechnic). One member (the London Borough of Richmond) recently left the network, preferring to go-it-alone using a package specifically tailored to local requirement by a commercial software house.

BLCMP has designed and implemented a computer system which utilizes the UK and US MARC databases and also produces records locally in the MARC format. A Selective Record Service is offered and the BLCMP Online Support Service (BOSS) supports comprehensive online cataloguing, access and acquisitions facilities. Output may be on cards, in book form or in microform. Tape output is also provided principally for users of CIRCO (the stand-alone circulation system). CIRCO's enquiry routines may be used to provide a measure of menu-driven local online cataloguing access via acronyms for author/title, class number and control number. Full public access software is currently at the specification stage and should be available in late 1984 with the first installation at Birmingham Polytechnic.[1]

Subscribers to BLCMP can obtain classified catalogues compiled by Dewey decimal, Library of Congress, Universal decimal or British catalogue of music classification schemes. Libraries may also opt to receive a subject index (see also page 107).

Since 1978, BLCMP has been responsible, under contract to the British Library, for BNB printed cards. These are automatically produced (by a computer bureau) from supplied magnetic tapes.

BLCMP's aim is to secure for its members the benefits of the latest technology whilst at the same time introducing increased individual library control over bibliographic information in catalogues.

SWALCAP (South-West Academic Libraries Cooperative Automation Project)

Like BLCMP, SWALCAP began in 1969. Financial support came from OSTI (the Office for Scientific and Technical

---

1 BLCMP update on services and systems / Tony Hall, Robert Watson
Vine (54) June 1984 11-15

Information, later the British Library Research and Development Department). As the name implies, its membership consists largely of university and polytechnic libraries, but one special library (the British Broadcasting Corporation Reference Library) is also a member, as is an 'academic-special library', the College of Librarianship Wales.

SWALCAP's present cataloguing service has been operational since 1978. The system is MARC compatible and SWALCAP encourages co-operation and a unity of approach among its members, but there are very few constraints upon the activities of individual libraries. Entries may be as brief or as full as each member library considers appropriate; output may be on COM, card or paper. Liverpool Polytechnic's COM catalogue, for instance, continues to include the keyword facility (see page 91) which was used prior to SWALCAP membership.

SWALCAP online cataloguing is menu-driven with access via acronyms or control numbers (see also page 47). Some libraries have attempted to use the circulation control subsystem for online public catalogue access. A stand-alone cataloguing system is, however, in process of development.

SWALCAP is a member of BLCMP and, if an item is not in the SWALCAP base, it is possible to order an offline search of the BLCMP files. A magnetic tape containing 'hits' is supplied to SWALCAP so that appropriate records can be made available to the requesting library. A merger between BLCMP and SWALCAP was proposed at one time but this did not materialize.

LASER (London And South Eastern library Region)
LASER originated in the 1930s as SERLS (the South-Eastern Regional Library System). The original functions of such regional systems were to facilitate the interlending of books among libraries in their area and via the National Central Library, to act as centres of bibliographic information and to maintain union catalogues. The LASER network as it is known today, however, dates from 1970 and has an involvement not only with interlending but also with cataloguing services and with other technology such as viewdata systems.

A LASER minicomputer supports the interlending and associated services and the union catalogue database contains well over one million bibliographic records which represent the 57 member libraries' stock of more than 40 million volumes. All members are located within the LASER geographic area.

During 1978 several members asked to be linked to the minicomputer system not only for interlending and reference purposes but also for current cataloguing/retrospective conversion services. LASER was already providing its members with retrospective catalogue records as a result of the conversion of its union catalogue into machine-readable form, and the provision of a current catalogue record service was a logical development. For cataloguing purposes a parallel database to that held on the LASER minicomputer is now maintained on a bureau mainframe. At the time of writing four libraries are taking the Selective Record Service for current cataloguing.

It was from work done by LASER, and its strong links with the British National Bibliography, that the retrospective UK MARC database extending back to 1950 was born. LASER also has a post 1900 retrospective extra-MARC database. LASER records have been used by an increasing number of public libraries — both members and non-members — as the basis of their files. A two-year programme to convert the records in the LASER base to AACR2 has just been completed.

LASER pioneered a form of union catalogue which is now used in other British regions, a microform catalogue listing ISBN's or BNB serial numbers with locations.

SCOLCAP (SCOttish Libraries Cooperative Automation Project)

The development of SCOLCAP began in 1973 when a group of Scottish librarians began to investigate the advantages of library automation and the opportunities it offered for co-operation among Scottish libraries. Activities began in 1976, when funds were made available by the British Library Research and Development Department.

'The SCOLCAP project's history over the past five years is proof, if proof were needed, that the path of automation is full of pitfalls ... development and full implementation of the system has been hung up on a succession of contractual difficulties.'[1] During this period, SCOLCAP member libraries

1 SCOLCAP *Vine* (54) June 1984 21

have made use of the LOCAS batch cataloguing service and have contributed to the SCOLCAP union database SCOLCAT. This core database is held on a mini-computer and consists of some three quarters of a million UK MARC, LC MARC and extra-MARC records, together with local data and holdings information. This base is intended to satisfy the majority of cataloguing requirements, while a link to BLAISE provides the further facility of online access to the whole range of MARC files. The contractual position has now been resolved and system acceptance was scheduled for the late summer of 1984.

The complete projected SCOLCAP package provides for online acquisitions, cataloguing, information retrieval and management information.

At present there are twenty full or associate members of SCOLCAP and this is expected to increase to around forty. Member libraries range from the large National Library of Scotland down through academic and public libraries to the smaller special library, eg the Advocates Library.

Cooperative Automation Group

It was clearly desirable to have some means of coordinating the work of the main networks, with a view to planned development, and in 1980 the Cooperative Automation Group (CAG) was formed under the auspices of the British Library. The membership of CAG comprises representatives from the British Library, all of the major networks, and nominees from Aslib, the Library Association, SCONUL (Standing Conference of National and University Libraries) and COPOL (Council of Polytechnic Librarians). The general aim of CAG was to ensure the most effective articulation of the services provided by the British Library and the library co-operatives in the interests of the library community at large.

At an early stage, the Group decided to focus upon the possibility of creating a common database which would enable users in the UK to have access to a much larger file of catalogue records than any of the participants could offer individually — a UK Library Database System (UKLDS).

UKLDS

It was envisaged that the UK Library Database System as recommended by CAG would have two principal applications:

firstly, to make bibliographic records available for cataloguing purposes; secondly, to provide locations for reference or inter-lending use. There were two major problems, the first relating to technical and operational difficulties and the second to the conflict that must inevitably exist within a particular co-operative between the interests of its own members and those of the wider library community. In an attempt to overcome the financial implications of the latter, whilst at the same time solving the former, support was sought from the Office of Arts and Libraries to facilitate the technical enhancement of the various systems to provide the necessary interfaces. However, no government money could be made available and CAG has found it necessary to evaluate other options. In a press release issued in July 1984, CAG concluded that:

'It is no longer a realistic objective to pursue the establishment of UKLDS in the way that was originally conceived. Instead, what is envisaged is a loose series of networking arrangements, resulting in the exchange of data between different parties on mutually agreed terms and conditions. In this way the cooperatives and the British Library will be free to make arrangements at their own pace with priorities that match their organisational objectives. CAG will thus formally cease to have as its objective the structured development of UKLDS, although it is expected that the networking arrangements will go a long way towards fulfilling one of the major aims of UKLDS, that of improving the sharing and accessibility of bibliographic records.'

CAG will continue to exist but the main force of work will shift to a Steering Group, consisting of representatives of the UK co-operatives and the British Library. This Group has undertaken to keep other members of CAG informed and to convene a meeting of the full Group should major policy matters arise for discussion.

Other networks of the UK
Those networks described above are the ones of particular interest to cataloguers in Britain but there are other services of indirect relevance.

Blackwell Technical Services (BTS) maintains an auto-mated network for serials control (PERLINE and its sub-systems) and monograph acquisition (BOOKLINE and its subsystems). Blackwell files can be interrogated online and, although the provision of dedicated cataloguing systems is outside the range of BTS services, the need to interface with cataloguing activity is recognized so that accumulated data may usefully be passed across.[1] MICA (MARC Interface for Cataloguing and Acquisitions) will write data to and from the MARC formats for monographs and serials. (Blackwell North America provide similar services in the United States, the two largest customers being the New York Public Library and the University of California at Berkeley.)

Pergamon online information services (Infoline) constitute a network of the Dialog (see page 176) type. Some of the databases provided are available elsewhere (eg COMPENDEX) whilst others are claimed to be exclusive (eg Electronic Publishing Abstracts).

Networks outside the US and UK
Although the brevity of this work precludes the detailing of developments world-wide, it must be stressed that networking is not confined to the US and the UK. The following examples are included in order to illustrate more general trends.

Australia — ABN
'The Australian Bibliographic Network (ABN) combines in effect the functions of an online cataloguing network, a national database, and a national union catalogue, in addition to providing the National Library of Canberra with an in-house cataloguing system.'[2]

ABN makes use of the Washington Library Network (WLN) software and the WLN LCMARC based file was retrospectively acquired. To this were added the National Library's AUSMARC and selected UK and CANMARC records. This formed the basis of a bibliographic file which now contains some three million records. Cataloguing information for material other than books, including audiovisual materials, is being added.

Online searches are command driven and a number of

1 Blackwells beaver away : FIBER, PERLINE and BOOKLINE / Phil Holmes, Angela Pacey, Taube Marks *Vine* (54) June 1984 22-28
2 ABN : a national cataloguing network / Judith Baskin, Warwick Cathro, Diana Dack *Vine* (53) April 1984 4-12

access points are provided including author, title or subject. Right hand truncation is possible and there is some Boolean capability. There are five levels of display from brief entries to full MARC format.

A participating library, after finding a relevant record in the database, can opt to accept it and simply add a holdings statement or to amend the record first before adding the statement.

There were upwards of 60 participants with leased lines in April 1984 (approximately 325 terminals connected) and the number of additional 'dial-up' customers is increasing rapidly.

Canada — UTLAS Inc (formerly University of Toronto Library Automation Systems)
This is a bibliographic utility which has been supplying computer-based systems, services, and products in both English and French since 1973. More recently, UTLAS has won clients in countries outside Canada, including the United States and Japan. With regard to the latter, the first high-speed data communications link between Canada and Japan was established in 1982. This allowed the Maruzen Company (one of Japan's largest book companies) and the International Christian University to connect online to UTLAS in Toronto.[1]

The online network includes over 330 institutions and members of consortia. More than 2,000 individual libraries receive services and products from the system. These services include: online cataloguing; name and subject authority control; retrospective conversion; upgrading of databases to AACR2 standard; acquisitions control (including fund accounting) and serials control; reference service support; and online public access catalogues. Book, card, and COM catalogues can be supplied, and also machine-readable records on magnetic tape. Other products include customized bibliographies, KWIC indexes, acquisitions lists, locally generated labels, and purchase orders. The database now contains well over 23 million records and includes files from the Library of Congress, the national libraries of Canada, France, and the UK, and the US National Library of Medicine.

Customers may opt to maintain a strictly private file on

1 UTLAS-Japan communications link / George Gorsline and Wyley L. Powell *Information technology and libraries* 2 (1) March 1983 33-34

the system but must subscribe to a shared-data concept in which copies of records created by them, minus local data, are added to the pool of cataloguing information available to users.[1]

UTLAS is the only Canadian utility with the concept of shared cataloguing data among participants, and is, therefore, a *de facto* national network.[2]

UTLAS has recently signed a joint marketing agreement with CL Systems Inc (CLSI — see also page 145). Under this agreement, CLSI will market UTLAS database products and services in the US, while UTLAS will market CLSI local library systems and services in Canada. In addition, UTLAS and CLSI plan to develop co-operatively new products which will facilitate the integration of the centralized and local automation approach for libraries.

Another recent development was the signing of an agreement in the spring of 1984 between the Quebec Ministère des Communications and UTLAS. Under this agreement, UTLAS has a Quebec partner with the exclusive right to offer UTLAS' services and products in that province. Machine-readable files created by existing Quebec customers of UTLAS will be replicated in Quebec while maintaining an automatic, interactive, and transparent link between the Quebec service centre and the UTLAS network. This creation of a Quebec node falls into UTLAS' long-term objective of distributive processing, ie decentralizing its services wherever possible. The technical feasibility of doing so is ensured by the new Tandem computer systems to which UTLAS has just converted.

The new Tandem systems offer UTLAS the technical flexibility to replicate its services anywhere in the world and to refine and expand still further its services and product offerings.

Netherlands — PICA
PICA is the Dutch national shared cataloguing network run from the Royal Library in the Hague. The network has 180 terminals spread over 30 locations by leased lines. Members include the Royal Library, seven university libraries, the

1 Cataloguing in Canada *International cataloguing* 11 (3) July/September 1982 28-32
2 *ibid.*

Dutch National Bibliography and the Dutch Documentation Centre. This last organization produces catalogue cards for some 900 public libraries. The database holds some three million plus records, including LC and UK MARC records. Locations are given for some two million of these. The online system is a mix of menu and command mode but access is somewhat restricted being 'based on the assumption that the enquirer will be working from book-in-hand.'[1]

PICA also supports acquisition, circulation control and inter-library lending.

A public access catalogue has been under development and this was planned for introduction in 1984.

One PICA member, the University of Utrecht, is also a Geac (see page 144) user. It therefore provides an interesting 'study of the potentially conflicting demands of belonging to a shared "national" system and meeting local needs via a local system.'[2] The library uses Geac for cataloguing and sees the main benefits of PICA 'not in its use as a shared cataloguing resource but in its interlending potential.'[3] Nevertheless, in compliance with government policy, the Universiy has agreed to put 10,000 records through PICA in 1984.

Sweden – LIBRIS (LIBRary Information System)
LIBRIS, centred upon the Royal Library, has been the major library automation project in Sweden. It began in 1972 and was primarily designed to meet the needs of Swedish research libraries. The database currently contains citations of the holdings of more than 100 such libraries. The cataloguing of an item is done at the library which first acquires it and the input is immediately available for online retrieval at all the libraries in the network. The central base also contains LCMARC and UKMARC records.

Sweden – BUMS (Bibliotekstjänst, Utlåningsoch Mediakontroll System)
This is a circulation and media control system developed by Bibliotekstjänst, the Swedish Libraries' Central Service Organization. At present, BUMS consists of two subsystems:

1 Dutch and Belgian library systems : a compendium / Derek Law
Vine (53) April 1984 38-42
2 *ibid.*
3 *ibid.*

a cataloguing system, which includes routines for recording, maintaining and retrieving information in the bibliographic database, and a circulation control system.

Catalogues are generated in microform, or on paper, and, apart from a library's main catalogue, it is possible to produce specialized lists from the data stored in the central files, eg lists of recent acquisitions, books in various foreign languages, books in local collections, etc.

Over 40 public library systems in Sweden, with a total of some 400 service points, make use of the BUMS service, mainly for the provision of microfiche catalogues. There is a planned online link with LIBRIS.

EURONET/DIANE

The EURONET concept had its beginnings in 1971 when the Council of Ministers of the European Community passed a resolution with a view to 'coordinating the action of the Member States regarding scientific and technical information and documentation'. The initial intent of the overall EURO-NET plan, which grew out of this resolution, was to utilize the international, national and specialized systems already in existence and bring them together under the control of one European agency. This was an ambitious project; the system took some time to become operational (1980) and it is still expanding and developing. DIANE (Direct Information Access Network for Europe) is the name that has been given to the ensemble of available information services and the name EURONET is now reserved for the telecommunication network only. The scale of development can be illustrated by the fact that in late 1980 the system included 16 hosts offering upwards of 100 databases and by 1983 there were circa 40 hosts with a corresponding increase in bases (approximately 400). Among the first suppliers, or hosts, was the British Library's BLAISE service. Extension of the network beyond the European Economic Community has been actively promoted.

Chapter Ten

The future

Technology
There is little doubt that, as circuit density increases, the
computer will continue to decrease in size; it will become
faster and more powerful as the design of circuitry gets even
more sophisticated; it will have a greater immediate access
and backing store capacity as new methods of storage are
developed; and it will become more user-friendly. The
computer user may not even have to 'operate' the machine,
in the accepted sense of the word, but merely converse with
it, using a voice-activated terminal.

Peripherals will improve, note the introduction of touch
terminals, and other significant developments are in the off-
ing such as the flat-screen monitor which can be hung on a
wall.

Links between computers will be more efficient and
cheaper to accomplish. The University of California Division
of Library Automation, for instance, is investigating the use
of packet radio (the marriage of radio and packet switching),
as an alternative to the expensive installation of dedicated
wiring, to transmit information between terminals and the
online catalogue.

Data will be passed from point to point at greater velocity.
New technology such as fibre optics (see Glossary), with
information being transferred at the speed of light, will
revolutionize the communication process. International
links will be improved.

The computer will become less costly and more common;
nearly every household will possess one, interlinked with
other devices such as the telephone and cable television to
provide two-way interaction with the outside world.

Catalogue access

One will therefore be able to access the library catalogue from the comfort of one's own fireside. Such access will be non-stop 24 hour access, seven days a week, and will relate not only to the local library catalogue but to indexes of other collections of information and also to the information itself.

The three major problems of the information transfer process are:

1 Discovering what information exists.

2 Discovering where this information may be obtained.

3 Obtaining the information.

Traditional cataloguing is concerned with the first two of these but Hopkins[1] maintains that the real revolution will come with the solution of the third problem, that of quickly obtaining desired information or desired documents in one format or another.

One of the technical facilities which will allow very fast access to information contained in documents is online interactive retrieval of full text. Writers such as Lancaster point to the 'growing cost and to the inefficiency of transmitting information in the form of paper.'[2] The time will come, these writers predict, when the composition, publishing and retrieval of information will be done electronically through online systems.

Full text retrieval is, of course, already possible. On page 192 will be found a simple example using a free text database system for DEC-10 and DEC-20 computers called 3RIP. The data in this instance consists of the works of Lewis Carroll. A search is being conducted for the details and actual text of the poem which the enquirer knows contains the words 'Brillig' and 'Slithy'.

Kilgour sees the most exciting prospect for the next several years as 'the integration of catalog and information supply functions, hereby it will be possible for the information seeker at his personal computer to obtain an item almost as rapidly as he can locate a catalog entry.'[3]

1 Technology and the future of libraries / Richard L. Hopkins *Argus* 9 (2) Mars-Avril 1980 41-51

2 *Towards paperless information systems* / F.W. Lancaster. — Academic Press, 1978

3 *The online catalog revolution* / Frederick G. Kilgour *op. cit.*

```
* BRILLIG AND SLITHY
Set 1: 2 hits in 1 record

* SHOW
POEMS records: / 1 /
Set 1: 1 record (format: 2)

Record 1   (POEMS:13, see also MIRROR:24)

Poem: JABBERWOCKY
Chapter 1: Looking-Glass House
Number of verses and lines: 7 and 28

Skip to next record? /YES/: N
Persons in the poem:
    Tove
    Borogove
    Rath
    Jabberwock
    Jubjub
    Bandersnatch

    'Twas brillig, and the slithy toves
      Did gyre and gimble in the wabe:
    All mimsy were the borogoves,
      And the mome raths outgrabe.

    "Beware the Jabberwock, my son!
      The jaws that bite, the claws that catch!
    Beware the Jubjub bird, and shun
      The frumious Bandersnatch!"

    He took his vorpal sword in hand:
      Long time the manxome foe he sought -
    So rested he by the Tumtum tree,
      And stood awhile in thought.
Continue? /YES/:
    And, as in uffish thought he stood,
      The Jabberwock, with eyes of flame,
    Came whiffling through the tulgey wood,
      And burbled as it came!

    One, two! One, two! And through and through
      The vorpal blade went snicker-snack!
    He left it dead, and with its head
      He went galumphing back.

    "And hast thou slain the Jabberwock?
      Come to my arms, my beamish boy!
    O frabjous day! Callooh! Callay!"
      He chortled in his joy.

    'Twas brillig, and the slithy toves
      Did gyre and gimble in the wabe:
    All mimsy were the borogoves,
      And the mome raths outgrabe.
```

Full text search in 3RIP Lewis Carroll database for poem containing words 'Brillig' and 'Slithy'

Although the storage of complete items and subsequent online access to particular sections is already possible (there are, for instance, several online encyclopaedias) the large scale storage of complete collections using a medium such as magnetic disc would require an enormous disc capacity and is not presently practicable. However, one storage device which *is* making the retrieval of actual documents from a collection feasible *now* is the optical digital disc. This 'will not replace the magnetic disk as a storage device'[1] but library materials, whether book, slide, map, manuscript, or whatever, can relatively easily and cheaply be transformed for storage in this way and then accessed as necessary, within a few seconds, via a terminal video system. Work of this nature is already being done in France, where public access to both national catalogues and actual material, via millions of home videotex terminals, is planned,[2] and also at the Library of Congress, where a pilot optical disc program has been in progress for some time.[3]

Digital optical discs can store information economically at very high densities. One 8 × 10½ inch book page occupies 54,000 square millimetres. This can be reduced to 70 square millimetres on 98 frame microfiche and to an amazing 3 to 6 square millimetres on optical disc.[4] At the Library of Congress information is input via a page scanner (or fiche scanner) which scans the material and stores the data temporarily on magnetic disc to allow quality review before writing to the optical disc. The optical discs are contained in a 'jukebox', which holds 100 discs, and when a user requests material the appropriate disc will be retrieved and the requested pages stored on a magnetic disc buffer for use. If the user wants a copy of the material, he or she may use the adjacent printer or may request an offline batch print.[5]

1 The reality of information storage, retrieval and display using video-discs / Julie Schwerin *Videodisc and optical disc* 4 (2) March/April 1984 113-121
2 Address by F. Reiner (Mediatheque, France) at *Information technology in the library/information school curriculum : an international conference (1983 : London)*
3 The Library of Congress optical disk pilot program : a report on the print project activities / Ellen Z. Hahn *Library of Congress information bulletin* 42 (44) October 31 1983 374-376
4 *ibid.*
5 *ibid.*

An input and output system is being developed to link the optical disc system with SCORPIO (see page 174). The LC pilot operation began in January 1984 and will extend through 1985.

The possibilities of the optical disc could have an effect not only on the storage of the actual material but also on the storage of indexes to these materials. The whole of the OCLC database, for instance, might be transferred to a few optical discs, the largest database of its kind in the world in an easily transportable form! To date it has taken a very large computer to distribute records online. If an optical disc drive could be linked to a microcomputer such as the IBM Personal, and such systems are already being developed, then the nature of distributed cataloguing as it is known today would be revolutionized. A movement could well take place, therefore, away from record supply and towards system supply complete with database.

Whether a catalogue is stored on optical disc or magnetic disc, 'access techniques should be simple and easy to use, with both intellectual and physical manipulation held to an absolute minimum.'[1] Kilgour, from whom the above quote is taken, believes that with such catalogues 'it will not be necessary to have extensive descriptive cataloging rule systems, such as the second edition of *Anglo-American cataloguing rules.*'[2] Other writers disagree: 'We must not give up almost 250 years of Anglo-American cataloging service for techno-logical sizzle. We must not limit the catalog. We must exploit the new technology to enhance its proper performance of its essential, historic and traditional functions.'[3]

A recent study of full and short entry catalogues under-taken by the Centre for Catalogue Research at the University of Bath[4] points to the advantages of the short entry and 'will doubtless encourage more libraries to use them in their online public access catalogs.'[5]

Whatever the view taken of short entry catalogues, Michael

1 The online catalog revolution / Frederick G. Kilgour *op. cit.*
2 *ibid.*
3 Must we limit the catalog? / Maurice J. Freedman *Library journal* 109 (3) February 15 1984 322-324
4 Full and short entry catalogues : library needs and uses / Alan Seal, Philip Bryant, Carolyn Hall. – Bath : University Library, 1982
5 Library automation & networking perspectives on three decades / Richard De Gennaro *op. cit.*

Gorman predicts, and this author hopes that he is right, that 'there will never be an AACR3.'[1] 'The next general cataloguing code will be a manual on how to create MARC records for the national online network. Those MARC records will be different to our present linear records in that they will be multi-dimensional and based on authority file concepts such as those partially established in the WLN system.'[2] The national network Gorman refers to is, of course, the United States national network which he sees as being 'an amalgamation of OCLC and RLIN which will be decreed by a commission set up by CLR, LC and ARL and formed to deal with the aftermath of RLIN's financial collapse.'[3]

Irrespective of the future of AACR2 and MARC, one thing seems sure — subject access must be improved. 'The CLR/OPAC survey . . . online catalog transaction log analyses, focussed group interviews and data and statistical reports from several libraries (including the Library of Congress and the University of California Library System) attest to the "fact" that the great majority of library users are performing *topical subject* searches, not author/title or known-item searches. This is the overwhelming finding from these studies. It was also the finding from some earlier catalog use studies, but this time the weight of the evidence cannot be ignored or unheeded.'[4]

Various ways have been suggested as to how this improvement may be achieved. Gorman states that 'in the field of subject access . . . we will see a move towards the simplification of shelf classification numbers, accompanied by a refinement of the use of classification in machine systems.'[5] Svenonius identifies a number of uses of classification in online retrieval systems of the future. These include the improvement of recall (the number of relevant documents produced in answer to an enquiry) and precision (a comparison of the recall, as defined above, with the total number of documents, relevant or irrelevant, produced by the search)

1 Technical services, 1984-2001 (and before) / Michael Gorman *Technical services quarterly* 1 (1/2) Fall/Winter 1983 65-71
2 *ibid.*
3 *ibid.*
4 A paradigm shift in library science / Pauline A. Cochrane *Information technology and libraries* 2 (1) March 1983 3-4
5 Technical services, 1984-2001 (and before) / Michael Gorman *op. cit.*

and the saving of the user's time in keying in search terms. In some areas of knowledge, perspective hierarchies can be used to contextualize the meaning of vague search terms, enabling the user to simulate in part the negotiation of a search request carried on by reference librarians. A further important use of traditional classification in online systems is to provide a structure for meaningful browsing.[1] One writer opinionates that 'there is not a very great future in the use of keywords, Boolean algebra, or LC subject headings in online searching. It is more likely that classification will be mandatory, perhaps of the type already begun by SMALLTALK.'[2] SMALLTALK is a user-friendly computer language which, in its early stages, was for use by children. It is of interest for subject analysis because it is based on a system of classification and makes use of the way that the human mind recognizes patterns.[3] A further possibility is the use of PRECIS (see also page 130). PRECIS is used in certain systems 'because it supplies more possible searching points than are provided by keywords and Boolean combinations. PRECIS supplies strings of terms, with relationships indicated both among the operators identifying single or multi-word terms themselves, and by the sequence (ie the string sequence) of these identified terms. PRECIS allows more places to look because the string strategy and the term strategy are built in as a part of its context-dependency aspect.'[4]

Integration

'The greatest virtue of automated database systems is that they permit a single file of information, once converted to machine-readable form, to serve different functions.'[5]

The integration of cataloguing with other operations such as acquisitions and circulation control has already been discussed and advocated. Where the latter is concerned, for instance, it should be possible for any online catalogue user and prospective borrower, whether an individual or an

1 Use of classification in online retrieval / Elaine Svenonius *Library resources and technical services* 27 (1) January/March 1983 76-80
2 Futuristic aspects of subject access / Phyllis A. Richmond *Library resources and technical services* 27 (1) January/March 1983 88-93
3 *ibid.*
4 *ibid.*
5 The future of the catalog : the library's choices / S. Michael Malinconico and Paul J. Fasana. *op. cit.*

institution, to ascertain in advance the answer to questions such as: Is the item that I have selected available? If not, when is it likely to be available? Such online interrogation facilities are already provided in a number of libraries.

It should eventually also be possible for the user to automatically transmit his/her request onwards whenever necessary to other libraries and information centres, or even to publishers or booksellers. Electronic order transmission has already begun, albeit on a small scale, in the US and the UK. Writers such as Bonk[1] maintain that increasing automation in the book trade and in libraries will lead to a new type of bookseller/library interface and relationship.

As previously indicated, the user will expect that the terminal that provides him/her with catalogue access will also provide access to other services. 'Catalogues will be the bibliographic component of a complex of interacting systems linked and presented to their users by sophisticated interface programs which will appear to the user of the systems to constitute one system.'[2] Thus the abstracting and indexing services, for example, which, although similar in nature, have developed independently from and are thus largely incompatible with automated cataloguing systems, will at last be 'integrated' with them. It should be possible to provide choices for the catalogue user between, for instance, a book on a particular subject or a recent periodical article.

Gorman advocates a radical review of serial publishing, one of his ideas being a unification of the indexing and abstracting process with an 'electronic' publishing process.[3] The computer has facilitated much improved control of serials, those incomplete items which are such a problem to the librarian. The future is certain to see some changes in the publishing and dissemination of this form of material and this will, in turn, have an effect on indexing technique.

Conclusion
Nobody can predict exactly what will happen in the next decade but we can be sure that the impact of the computer

1 Integrating library and book trade automation / Sharon C. Bonk *Information technology and libraries* 2 (1) March 1983 18-25
2 Technical services, 1984-2001 (and before) / Michael Gorman *op. cit.*
3 Mutating the genome / Michael Gorman *Cataloging and classification quarterly* 3 (2/3) Winter 1982/Spring 1983 19-25

will become ever more pronounced. These are exciting times for the catalogue producer. The function of the catalogue remains unaltered but the means of implementing that function grow ever more sophisticated and the basic function may ultimately be enhanced by an ability to retrieve not only relevant document citations but the actual documents themselves. The catalogue is a key to the doors of knowledge; in the past it has not always been the most efficient of devices but, computerized, it should become a golden key with a golden future.

Further reading

Because of the speed with which events are happening, the major source of further reading should be the periodical literature as indicated in the Author's Note on page vii. The monographic literature of the computer is vast and it would be impossible to cite all of the books which might provide relevant additional and further background reading. The sample titles below are indicative of what is available. The list is confined to a few of the many works published in the last five years which the author has personally examined and found to be useful. It includes both texts which deal with the computer in general and texts which concentrate on the use of the computer in library and information work.

Bradbeer, Robin
    The computer book : an introduction to computers and computing / Robin Bradbeer, Peter de Bono, Peter Laurie, with additional material by Susan Curran and David Allen. — British Broadcasting Corporation, 1983.
Cassel, Don
    Introduction to computers and information processing / Don Cassel, Martin Jackson. — Reston, 1980.
Davis, Charles H
    Guide to information science / Charles H Davis and James E Rush. — Greenwood Press, 1979 ; Library Association, 1980.
Fosdick, Howard
    Computer basics for librarians and information scientists / Howard Fosdick. — Information Resources Press, 1981.
Fry, T F
    Beginner's guide to computers / T F Fry. — 2nd ed. — Newnes, 1983.
Hagler, Ronald
    The bibliographic record and information technology / Ronald Hagler and Peter Simmons. — American Library Association, 1982.
Hildreth, Charles R
    Online public access catalogs : the user interface / Charles R Hildreth. — OCLC, 1982.

Introducing the online catalogue : papers based on seminars held in 1983 / edited by Alan Seal. — Bath University Library Centre for Catalogue Research, 1984.

Lovecy, Ian
Automating library procedures : a survivor's handbook / Ian Lovecy. — Library Association, 1984.

Rowley, J E
Computers for libraries / J E Rowley. — Bingley, 1980.

Sager, Donald J
Public library administrators' planning guide to automation / Donald J Sager. OCLC, 1983.

Sommerville, Ian
Information unlimited : the applications and implications of information technology / Ian Sommerville. — Addison-Wesley, 1983.

Willis, Jerry
Computers for everybody/ Jerry Willis and Meri Miller. — 3rd ed. — Dilithium Press, 1984.

Zorkoczy, Peter
Information technology : an introduction / Peter Zorkoczy. Pitman, 1982.

Index

This index was produced with computer assistance. The text was examined sequentially and as index entries were selected they were input to a machine held file on a DEC-20 mainframe. When all necessary entries had been made, the file was sorted alphabetically by the computer and then edited before being printed out for use as the basis of the final index.

The abbreviation *def* indicates that the page number which follows contains a definition of the indexed term.

Page numbers in bold type relate to illustrations.

When titles of documents are indexed, these are italicized.

Acronyms, names of computer packages, names of networks, programming statements and online search commands are normally capitalized.

Author index entries are included for references works cited in footnotes. When an item is referred to more than once, only the first relevant page is given.